DRINK AUSTRALIA PTY LTD
Published by Drink Australia
PO Box 873 Newtown,
NSW 2042, Australia

First Published 2003

A CIP catalogue record for this publication is available from the National Library of Australia.

ISBN 0-646-42114-X

Title: Liquid Kitchen, The
Author: Hayden Wood
Designer/Photographer: Esmeralda Wood
Pre-Press: George Maniatis - Spinninghead
Contributing Food Photography:
Jeremy Simons - Vivid Productions (pp 60-61)
Michael Cook (pp 106-107)

Printed by Toppan Printing Hong Kong Co. Ltd.

Those at risk from the affects of salmonella food poisoning should consult their doctor with any concerns about consuming raw eggs.

Those who may be susceptible to reactions from nuts including peanut oil should be mindful of some of the products used in these recipes.

www.barequip.com
www.mondobartender .com

the liquid kitchen

the liquid kitchen for esmeralda

contents

the liquid kitchen

When I was 10 years old I made the move from spending my afternoons in front of the TV to experimenting in the kitchen. Though not many original food recipes were created, it did make me realise that my passions were liquid concoctions.

With good old Kiwi ingenuity I am proud to share with you my experiences, inspirations and recipes as a professional bartender - ideally packaged up for The Liquid Kitchen accompanied by some great food from some of my cheffy mates in Sydney.

This is not a standard recipe book for bartenders wanting to know every classic and popular drink out there. Treat this as a snapshot to early 21st Century drink recipes influenced by a dash of current popular flavours and past classics.

Whether you read or flick through this book,
I hope you gather inspiration to venture into your own kitchen
to conjure up some tasty drinks
using the dusty remnants of your liquor cabinet.

So pull out the bag of lemons, don't be afraid of the sugar and be generous with the vodka - it's all about adding confidence to your recipe repertoire that will soon have your house buzzing with a hive of activity centred around you and The Liquid Kitchen.

woody

in a perfect world

The greatest way to live with a liquid kitchen is to enjoy a balanced diet of food with alcohol. The key to responsible drinking is simply attitude. Being a great host is looking after your friends and family with a genuine sense of care for their wellbeing. Reflect this in your hospitality and your circle of friends will grow to include extremely interesting and exciting people. As I like to say, what goes around comes around.

Here are a few pointers to consider when organising an event that includes cocktails:
Work out your guest list and roughly how long everyone will be drinking for. Then prepare adequate arrival food and a more substantial meal for later.

Always have food available throughout the night. Chips and dips simply don't cut the mustard; so get some inspiration from some of our friends' suggestions at the end of each chapter.

Stay in control of your party and don't fall subject to an early pass out. This runs a very dead vibe through what should be a great occasion.

Get your friends enthusiastic about making their own drinks. Get the mood going with some pre-made drinks ready to go so it doesn't get too crowded in the kitchen - check out the punches chapter.

When your party's in full swing take a big jug of cold infused water around and pour up some refreshments. Generally people don't think to dilute a night of cocktails with water, so don't wait to be asked . . . get in there! To stay in control of your party, consume one glass of water to every cocktail.

Do me a favour at your next cocktail party,
please put as much effort into the food as you do the drinks.

I've included a tasty selection of great food suggestions at the end of each chapter by some of my friends, including Lyndey Milan, Longrain, Katering and Cherry Bim.

eeeeeeeeeeeeeeeeeeeeeeeeeeeeeeeee
eeeeeeeeeeeeeeeeeeeeeeeeeeeeeee

essentials

The liquid kitchen doesn't need every fancy and hip appliance to make it happen. I used to live in an apartment that had a fridge the size of a large shoe box, and a kitchen to match. Of course I didn't have allot of supplies back then because I simply didn't have the space, but I made do with the essentials listed below.

essential supplies

Hard - vodka, rum, gin, tequila, liqueurs, cognac and champagne

Dry - napkins, straws, cinnamon, cloves, tea, coffee, chocolate, salt, vanilla pods, ginger, and sugar. When considering sugar for your drinks, think that sugar is to drinks what salt is to food.

Wet - pineapple juice, orange juice, cranberry juice, ruby red grapefruit juice, lemon juice, lime cordial, sugar syrup, milk, cream and ice

Fresh - lemons, limes, oranges, mint, berries, seasonal friut

Soft - soda water, lemonade, ginger beer

tools

These are the basic tools you'll need for most of the recipes listed in this book. I feel that in this case just grab what ever suits you.

- Jugs for holding juices
- Large sealable bottles for concentrated mixers
- Bowls for garnishes and holding chopped fruit, and large spoons or tongs
- A good blender
- Pots large and small
- Large ice bucket or plastic tub for your ice
- Large chopping board and a few sharp knives big or small plus a rinder for garnish
- Crushing stick / French rolling pin
- Shaker base that fits over your glasses so you can shake the mix up
- All sorts and different shapes and sizes of glassware
- Tea towels to clean and for crushing ice
- Spirit measure plus pour spouts for pouring control

preparation

It is essential that you organise your drinks area. Line up your bowls of fruit close to where you are going to prepare the drinks.

Most people may not like to use their hands to touch the fruit,
so keep some large spoons or tongs handy.

Get a French rolling pin/crush stick to crush fruit and to make crushed ice.

Find a decent sized ice bucket. One of the biggest pitfalls in home bars is the size of the ice bucket, so don't be afraid of cleaning up the laundry bucket and lining it with a rubbish bag to hold your ice. It makes things run much more smoothly throughout the night.

glassware

Presuming that your bar needs a selection of glassware to suit the kind of drinks you're inclined to make - such as: wine in a wine glass, spirits in old fashions and cocktails in cocktail glasses - can be a little daunting.

Well, I'm glad to break it to you that it just doesn't have to be that way. I have seduced Margaritas from tin cups, felt suave drinking Martinis served in pints and devoured breakfast smoothies straight from the blender. It simply doesn't matter how it's served so long as you're happy with the end result.

Glassware does always have a certain suitability when it comes to presentation and most people find it very hard to drink a tankard of Martini. Many of the drinks... are served in their appropriate glass: for example, Martinis in a martini glass; the Margaritas in a margi glass; and of course, long drinks in highballs and short drinks in lowballs.

My suggestion is to simply follow the style of glass featured in each recipe, and where you don't have it or can't get any, make do with what you have.

ice

Ice is essential to a bar what flour is to a bakery. It forms the base for most of the other ingredients in cold drinks. To have only a small amount of ice at your party is asking for trouble.

Although ice comes in many shapes and sizes it can be found at almost every service station in the world. When buying ice, allow 30 drinks to every 5kg bag, and if it won't fit in your freezer, this rule of thumb should also allow for melting should you keep it in a tub or sink.

Always use lots of ice in cold drinks.

The idea of using a few cubes is not only skimping on your presentation, it also means that the drink gets warmer faster, melting the ice which dilutes the flavour. To keep everything tasting great and looking good use loads of ice, and I mean loads - fill them to the rim and then some - keep it cool, clean and clear.

Here are a couple of terms used throughout the book that relate to the way ice is used.

on the rocks
Just fill your glass full of ice.

chilling a glass
Fill your glass with ice and remove the ice just before you pour your drink.

served up
After chilling your glass, pour your drink into the glass - a drink served without ice.

frozen drink
The amount of cubed ice that fills one glass will be the right amount for blending one frozen drink.

basic method - crushing ice

Add one scoop of ice to a clean tea towel. Wrap the ice up and bash it with a rolling pin. Scoop the crushed ice onto the top of your drink, or for a frappé fill your glass before required ingredients. Crushed ice makes any drink appear refreshing.

ice safety

Because it's mostly transparent it can very easily conceal the contents of broken glass. It's with the utmost importance that I stress the danger of using a glass to scoop ice. It's so easy to use a plastic scoop or cocktail shaker base instead of a glass. To do this ensures you won't chip or break your glass in the ice bucket and ruin a perfectly good tub of ice.

Furthermore, if you break a glass near the ice bucket and can't be sure that pieces of glass have made their way into the ice, just to be sure for yours and your friends' safety, throw it away and get a fresh bag. Sipping on a shard of glass can cause disastrous health problems!

essential methods

build

Building a drink is by and large the most simple method to make a drink. Pour the listed ingredients over ice in the desired glass. For more on building (see p 64).

muddling

Muddling is the method of extracting juice and oils from ingredients to add flavour to a drink. After crushing the ingredients, add ice and spirits or mixers before shaking in a cocktail can. Serve without straining the ingredients. For more on crushing (see p 41).

stir

The method of stirring allows the ingredients (to mix and chill) with the option of diluting the drink with more stirring, or leaving the drink undiluted with less stirring. Just add the ingredients to an ice-filled shaker or mixing glass and stir the ingredients before either straining into a chilled cocktail glass, or leaving the ice in the drink. Ten revolutions will provide a chilled, but limited, drink dilution. For more on stirring (see p 124).

shake

Add the listed ingredients to an ice filled cocktail shaker. Seal the shaker and then shake vigorously. This chills the ingredients and mixes them well. Now you can either strain the ice from the finished drink or simply pour with the ice into the desired glass. For more on shaking (see p 112).

blend

Add the listed ingredients to a blender with equal ice to the capacity of the glass. Before blending make sure the lid is on and you apply pressure to the blender cup to keep it on the motor base. Remove the cup and shake the ingredients before blending a second time to ensure all the ingredients are consistantly mixed. For more on blending (see p 112).

infuse

Add all your ingredients to a large pot or bowl. Some recipes require heating prior to the second stage. Then leave the mix to sit for 24-48 hours before straining off the solids and bottling. For more on infusing (see p 84).

steep

Pre-heat your teapot for two minutes with hot water and remove the water just before adding all your ingredients. Boil your water and prepare your tea Add your tea to the pot and leave for 5 - 7 minutes or as the recipe requires before serving. For more on steeping (see p 158).

draw

Firmly press the coffee into the handle cup with a round flat press tool allowing around 5mm of clearance from the lip of the handle cup. Ensure the machine has reached the right temperature and there is adequate water in the tank. Before making your first cup, run some water through the machine without the group handle in place. Fit the handle in the group and draw your brew. For more on coffee (see p 174).

mixers and garnish

planning ahead with mixers and garnish

Back in the days when I began experimenting with mixed drinks in the kitchen and not in the bar, I found myself getting into all sorts of trouble and mess. My drinks always tasted different even though I repeated the same recipe from one day to the next . . . so I formulated this rule for ensuring the perfectly balanced drink.

The rule of thirds applies:
1/3rd alcohol to 2/3rd's mixers.

Organising most of your ingredients before everyone arrives is the key to a successful cocktail fiesta. Don't be put off by the idea that you're not satisfying everyone with a large selection of drinks on the menu. Think of it like this: some like it fruity, some like it sweet and some a little sour. All of which you can easily create by adding - or not adding for that matter - a squeeze of lime or lemon.

So, ideally, choosse two or three cocktails and get everything prepped before your guests arrive.

As I always say, it's 9/10th's preparation
or it's not worth a tin of fish.

In this chapter I show you how to make a great range of mixers to suit any palate - from the essential Bloody Mary mix to the beloved Piña Colada mix. I also cover a whole load of garnishes to ensure you have a great-looking drink.

mixers

Mixers are the non-alcoholic ingredients found in mixed drinks and cocktails. They can include a simple ingredient like pineapple juice. On the other hand, if you mix pineapple juice with a range of other ingredients you can create something as tempting as a Piña Colada!

basic method - mixer prep

Prepare your pot, jugs or blender. Combine the ingredients in the blender and whiz until all the solids are smooth and thoroughly blended. Mixers like half 'n' half can be stirred or shaken in a bottle. Transfer the ingredients into your jug or bottle and chill in the fridge before serving.

Stir or shake the ingredients before using for the first time and if you have stored the ingredients (for any length of time) over a day, check the freshness by smelling before adding to your drink.

making piña colada mix

sugar syrup

Sugar syrup can easily be mistaken for a complicated and confusing concoction. It is a combination of 50% water to 50% sugar. Sugar syrup is a great ingredient to have on-hand, not only for many of this book's recipes but also for cooking.

Makes 1Lt / 33½oz, or approximately 50 crush drinks (see p 39)
500g / 16½oz white sugar
500ml / 16½oz hot water

Stir the ingredients in a pot on a medium heat before pouring into a bottle.

sweet 'n' sour

Sweet 'n' sour is an important ingredient in creating Margaritas, Daiquiris, Kamikazes, Sidecars and a multitude of other drinks. In fact, it provides consistency and ease-of-use to many of the fruit based drinks listed in this book.

Makes 1Lt / 33½oz, or approximately 16 drinks
250ml / 8½oz fresh lemon or lime juice
750ml / 25oz sugar syrup

Stir the ingredients in a jug or container.

half 'n' half

This mixer is not as heavy as pure cream. So drinks that include half 'n' half don't make you feel like you've just swallowed a cow's udder.

Makes 1Lt / 33½oz, or approx 16 drinks
500ml / 16½oz cream
500ml / 16½oz milk

Stir the ingredients in a jug or container.

bloody mary mix

The Bloody Mary is a lifesaver at breakfasts, brunches and other social gatherings where you need something hot and spicy. Just have vodka on ice ready and top it up with this tangy mixer to satisfy any hangover pang.

Makes 1Lt / 33½oz, or approximately 12 drinks

1 tablespoon Tabasco

3 tablespoons Worcestershire sauce

1 teaspoon horseradish or hot mustard

1 lime, juiced

1 tablespoon sweet sherry

celery salt, salt and pepper to taste

900ml / 30oz tomato juice

Blend the ingredients thoroughly before transferring to a jug or container.

bloody wasabi mix

Makes 1Lt / 33½oz, or approximately 12 drinks

2 tablespoons wasabi paste

1 lime, juiced

1 tablespoon sake

celery salt, salt and pepper to taste

900ml / 30oz tomato juice

Blend the ingredients thoroughly before transferring to a jug or container.

bloody thai mix

Mkaes 1Lt / 33½oz, or approximately 12 drinks

3 tablespoons soy sauce

3 medium sized chillies, chopped

2 teaspoons ginger, chopped

1 small clove garlic

1 lime, juiced

3 large fresh basil leaves

4 tablespoons sugar syrup

celery salt, salt and pepper to taste

900ml / 30oz tomato juice

Blend the ingredients thoroughly before transferring to a jug or container.

piña colada mix

One of the most popular cocktails in the world can turn into a disaster if you don't know the measurements. Traditionally a built drink (see p 68) and not blended, the mix itself needs to be blended and then stored in a jug, so all you need to do is add rum and you're away.

Makes 1Lt / 33½oz, or approximately 12 drinks

½ mango, skinned, pitted and diced

3 x 1cm thick pineapple slices, skinned and diced

350ml / 11½oz coconut milk, tinned

6 tablespoons caster sugar

1 lime or lemon, squeezed

500ml / 16½oz pineapple juice

Blend the ingredients thoroughly before transferring to a jug or container.

concentrated mixer

I usually use concentrated mixers in Daiquiris, Margaritas, Kamikazes and Sidecars. Some of these mixers are reduced in a pot to caramelize and concentrate the flavours.

basic recipe

To make a concentrated mixer, add any fruits and ingredients, including sugar, to a pot and heat for approximately 30 minutes. Allow the ingredients to cool before blending into a purée.

basic method

Prepare all your fruit and ingredients. Some skins may be best left on the fruit - best to check the recipe. Heat a pot to a high temperature and add the fruit, water and sugar. Continually stir for around three minutes so as not to burn or stick to the pot. Add the remaining ingredients and leave uncovered to reduce for a further 30 minutes.

Allow the ingredients to cool before blending and make sure the lid is tightly sealed as even warm ingredients will increase the pressure of a sealed blender when it is in motion. Pour the concentrate into a sealable bottle for easy use and chill in the fridge before use.

For clear concentrated mixers such as lemongrass syrup, cook the lemongrass stems in sugar syrup (see p 25) and strain. Pour the concentrate into a sealable bottle. Do not blend.

For a range of recipes and drinks to make with concentrated mixers - take a look in the Daiquiris, Margaritas, Kamikazes and Sidecars chapter (see pg 108).

caramelized apple cinnamon mix

Makes 500ml / 16½oz, or approximately 16 drinks

5 large granny smith apples, cored and chopped, skins still on

2 cups brown sugar

3 cups water

3 tablespoons cinnamon, ground

Follow the basic method (see p 28). Chill in the fridge before use.

quince mango mix

Makes 500ml / 16½oz, or approximately 16 drinks

5 quince cored, chopped, skins still on

2 mangoes, skinned and chopped

2 cups brown sugar

3 cups water

Blend the fresh mango with the cooked quince concentrate (see basic method p 28). Store in a bowl for easy serving with a spoon or use a plastic squeeze bottle. Chill in the fridge before use.

vanilla tangerine mix

Makes 500ml / 16½oz, or approximately 16 drinks

5 tangerines, peeled and chopped

2 vanilla pods, split

2 cups white sugar

3 cups water

Follow the basic method (see p 28). Remove the vanilla pod before blending. Chill in the fridge before use.

mango lychee mix

Makes 500ml / 16½oz, or approximately 16 drinks

2 tins of lychees

2 mangoes

2 cups sugar

3 cups water

Blend the fresh mango and lychee with the sugar and water. Store in a bowl for easy serving with a spoon, or use a plastic squeeze bottle. Chill in the fridge before use.

raspberry mint mix

Makes 500ml / 16½oz, or approximately 16 drinks

3 punnets raspberries

1 large watermelon slice

2 cups brown sugar

2 cups water

½ cup mint, chopped

Blend the fresh raspberries, watermelon and mint with the sugar and water. Store in a bowl for easy serving with a spoon, or use a plastic squeeze bottle. Chill in the fridge before use.

pineapple mint mix

Makes 500ml / 16½oz, or approximately 16 drinks

½ fresh pineapple

2 cups raw sugar

2 cups water

½ cup mint, chopped

Blend the fresh pineapple and mint with the sugar and water. Store in a bowl for easy serving with a spoon, or use a plastic squeeze bottle. Chill in the fridge before use.

lychee lemongrass mix

Makes 500ml / 16½oz, or approximately 16 drinks

juice from 2 tins of lychees

3 lemongrass stems, chopped

1 cup white sugar

2 cups water

Blend the lychees with a cooked lemongrass concentrate (see method p 25). Store in a bowl for easy serving with a spoon, or use a plastic squeeze bottle. Chill in the fridge before use.

raspberry plum mix

Makes 500ml / 16½oz, or approximately 16 drinks

3 punnets raspberries

5 dark plums

2 cups brown sugar

2 cups water

Follow the basic method (see p 28). Chill in the fridge before use.

peachy rose mix

Makes 500ml / 16½oz, or approximately 16 drinks

5 large peaches, peeled and pitted

2 tablespoons rosewater

2 cups white sugar

3 cups water

Follow the basic method (see p 28). Chill in the fridge before use.

simple garnish

Garnishes provide decoration and sometimes the final touch of flavour that can finish off a drink. Drinks with enormous garnishes embarrass me. They may as well have stuffed a whole Mardi Gras on the rim of the glass with the time it took to get it together. I like to keep my garnishes simple and tidy.

basic method - garnish prep

Use a clean chopping board and sharp knife. Have some bowls and plates ready to store the garnish. A good plastic squeeze bottle can be a great asset to the garnish buff.
Try and use fresh fruit free from blemishes and remember to wash your fruit before cutting to remove any grime.

If you are using fruit that requires preparation eg. limes, assess roughly how many drinks are going to be made using this garnish and check the yield note beside each listed garnish to work out how many drinks to prepare.

For dry garnishes eg. salt, coconut or chocolate, keep these a short distance away from the wet area so they don't spoil with drink spills. Garnishes like mint can be kept fresh in a glass with ice.

coconut, chopped nuts and chocolate flakes

citrus wedge

Citrus wedges add the final touch of presentation and flavour to a drink. The average wedge holds approximately 10ml/¼oz of juice, so if you find your drink is a little on the sweet side, a simple squeeze of a wedge will balance this out. Also, inserting a small cut through the flesh of the fruit allows you to place the wedge on the rim of the glass so the drinker can choose to add the squeeze to the drink or not.

1 lime yields 8 wedges
Top and tail your fruit removing approx 5mm/¼inch from either end. Cut through the centre from top to bottom creating two halves. Now cut four quarters from each half.

citrus wheel

Wheels are almost always used as ornamental garnishes. The cut in the side of the garnish allows for easy placement on the rim of the glass.

1 lime yields 5 wheels
Top and tail your fruit removing approx 5mm/¼inch from either end. Make a cut on one side of the fruit half way through from top to bottom. Cut the fruit into 5mm/¼inch sized wheels.

citrus rind

Citrus rind can be cut thicker for drinks like the Old Fashioned (see p 72) by using a knife as opposed to the rind cutter as shown. Long rinds can be curled by wrapping them on the handle of a spoon - this gives a very groovy spiral effect.

1 orange yields 10 rind garnishes
Using a small sharp knife or a rind cutter peel the skin from the fruit in 10ml/½inch wide strips. Trying to leave as much of the pith on the fruit as possible, cut the rind into 20ml/¾inch strips. Trim the edges of the strip to neaten the garnish.

chocolate topping

Using a squeeze bottle lay your pattern inside your glass. For a chocolate spider web lay your base pattern on the top of your drink. Drag a toothpick through the drink to achieve the desired patterned results.

chocolate discs

Over two pans of hot water melt chocolate slowly in two separate pots, with no added water or milk (half a bar of white chocolate and half and bar of dark chocolate). Once melted and prior to cooling, lay out on a baking tray a sheet of greaseproof paper where you can shape the chocolate into a disk, star or even letter shapes. This garnish can bring a simple drink alive.

additional garnishes

Salt, roasted almonds, sugar, cinnamon, nutmeg, hundreds and thousands, lime wedges, kiwi fruit wheels, rose petals, sliced star fruit, lemongrass slithers and pineapple leaves.

cccccccccccccccccccccccccccc

cccccccccccccccccccccccccccc

crush drinks

The brilliant thing about crush drinks - otherwise known as crushers, stick drinks and even stickies - is that these little babies are really easy to make and even easier to drink. I first came across the concept of muddling or crushing drinks from old cocktail books by Peter Jackson. Muddling an orange slice and a cherry in the bottom of your glass was the base to making an Old Fashioned cocktail, one of the long lost golden oldies of classic bourbon cocktails (see p 72). I was then reintroduced to the method when I first came to Sydney in the mid 90's and worked in a Latin American bar in The Rocks called Vivaz.

It wasn't until I was in Milan, while working for Coca Cola that I really got down and dirty with these drinks. Some friends dragged me out to a bar called Volo where they were using an enormous stick for bashing the ice in bags to break it up. So to accommodate everyone's thirst, I was invited to make some drinks... and to cut a long story short, we tried every fruit combination under the sun.

This traditional Brazilian method has been around since time immemorial. The national drink of Brazil, the Caipiriñha - was born using limes, Cachaça and raw sugar from plentiful local sugarcane plantations. Cachaça is a rum-like spirit made from distilled fermented sugar cane. Although its popularity and availability is growing in the west you can just as easily substitute it with a good rum like Havana Club.

All you need is an abundant selection of fresh seasonal fruits, some sugar and a little vodka to whip up a range of cocktails that have made places like Longrain in Sydney, Volo in Milan and Momo in London the talk of the town - all in your own kitchen.

So, here are some unbelievably refreshing drinks that are a cinch!

basic crush drink recipe

Half fill a 360ml / 12oz glass with:

fresh fruit

2-3 tablespoons caster sugar

15ml / ½oz sugar syrup (a good dash)

fill the glass with lots of ice

60ml / 2oz spirit, fruit juice, yoghurt or champagne

basic ingredients

So you can get an idea of quantities I've prepared the following:

6 limes make 4 Caipiroskas

1 punnet of strawberries make 4 Propagandas

2 nectarines make 4 Exoticas

2 bottles of spirit make 23 drinks with 60ml or 2oz in each drink

500g of caster sugar (more than enough for two gatherings of four people)

pre-make at least 700ml / 23½oz of sugar syrup

fruity mango and strawberries

basic crush method

Prepare sugar syrup (see p 25). Chop plenty of fruit up into crushable chunks and store in bowls. Leave citrus fruit skins on so oils can add to the drinks' flavour. Wash mint leaves and keep on ice for freshness. Store backup fruit in the fridge in case of a shortage when it gets busy.

Put the chopped fruit, caster sugar and sugar syrup in a glass. Then use a crush stick/French rolling pin to crush it down until you have a juicy mash/pulped flavour component. Fill the glass with ice and the listed spirit/s. Shake all ingredients.

If your cocktail shaker won't fit over your glass, crush the ingredients in the cocktail shaker and then pour it into your glass.

which is a caipiroska or caipiriñha?

I always used to get the names of the Caipiroska and Caiprinha mixed up. So let me tell you about Oscar (a fictitious character I have yet to put a face to) who comes from Russia, as does a lot of vodka.

So, Oscar is like caipirOSKA,
and caipriñha is the Brazilian one with rum.

Now I don't mix them up.

caipiroska

Makes 1 drink

½ glass fresh limes, chopped and skins left on

3 teaspoons caster sugar

20ml / ¾oz sugar syrup (see p 25)

ice

60ml / 2oz seriously ... vodka

Crush and then shake with ice. Pour into your glass.

caipiriñha

Makes 1 drink

½ glass fresh limes, chopped and skins left on

3 teaspoons caster sugar

20ml / ¾oz sugar syrup (see p 25)

ice

60ml / 2oz of Cachaça or Havana Club Silver dry rum

Crush and then shake with ice. Pour into your glass.

cha cha

For the person who likes the sweeter things in life this is most definitely the cocktail of choice.

Makes 1 drink

½ glass fresh pineapple and orange, chopped

2 teaspoons caster sugar

20ml / ¾oz sugar syrup (see p 25)

ice

30ml / 1oz Havana Club Silver dry rum

30ml / 1oz of Midori Melon liqueur

Crush and then shake with ice. Pour into your glass and garnish with pineapple leaves.

exotica

To my mind, it is better named erotica. Nectarines are a big favourite in our house, and in summer they are consumed by the box-load. I like to leave the skin on, especially if you can get the redness coming through as it makes the drink look very inviting. A good alternative to nectarines are strawberry mangos (named after the hint of strawberry flavour). This drink looks wonderful with the contrast of yellow flesh and bright red-orange skin pieces. The trick to making this cocktail light and fluffy is a teaspoon of egg white (see p 205), which once shaken creates a frothy attractive top.

Makes 1 drink

½ glass nectarines, chopped

½ fresh passionfruit

2 teaspoons caster sugar

20ml / ¾oz sugar syrup (see p 25)

ice

60ml / 2oz seriously ... vodka

Crush and then shake with ice. Pour into your glass.

crushed margarita

This is my style of Margarita. Easy to make and looks great. If you like salt on the rim of your drinking glass (see p 207), then do all the crushing in a separate glass and then pour it into the salt-rimmed glass.

Makes 1 drink
½ glass fresh limes, chopped
2 teaspoons caster sugar
20ml / ¾oz sugar syrup (see p 25)
ice
45ml / 1½oz Jose Cuervo tequila
15ml / ½oz Cointreau

Crush and then shake with ice. Pour into your glass and garnish with a lime wedge.

melon mint

Thanks to the abundance of huge watermelons in Australia, I never have difficulty making this drink any time of the year. Rock melons or honeydew melons make exceptional substitutes.

A good mate of mine, 'Big J' gave us a cutting of chocolate mint (it tastes like an after dinner mint) which makes a very unique alternative to standard mint as does spearmint.

Makes 1 drink
5 watermelon chunks
5 mint leaves, crushed and ripped
2 teaspoons caster sugar
ice
20ml / ¾oz sugar syrup (see p 25)
60ml seriously ... vodka

Crush and then shake with ice. Pour into your glass.

mojito

This traditional Cuban drink is great with a late lunch. It's a wonderful way to bring out the freshness in any food, whether hot or cold. I have only seen this drink served in a tall glass but you can just as easily make up a jug by multiplying the ingredients by four.

Makes 1 drink
½ glass fresh limes, chopped and skins left on
5 mint leaves, washed and ripped
3 teaspoons caster sugar
20ml / ¾oz sugar syrup (see p 25)
60ml / 2oz Havana Club Silver dry rum
ice
soda water, to top

Crush and then shake with ice. Pour into your glass and leave enough room for soda water to top. If preparing a jug mix the soda thoroughly to ensure a consistent flavour before serving.

mojito

propaganda

As the word suggests, this is a very persuasive drink for someone who is looking at presenting their guests with some after-dinner options. I find this drink works particularly well as a substitute for dessert - though I usually end up having both!

Makes 1 drink
5 strawberries, pruned and chopped
2 teaspoons caster sugar
20ml / ¾oz sugar syrup (see p 25)
ice
30ml / 1oz seriously ... pinky vodka
30ml / 1oz Chambord

Crush and then shake with ice. Pour into your glass. Strawberries can have a very tart flavour around wintertime so taste the fruit to determine whether or not it needs a little more sugar syrup or Chambord.

yin yang

This is one of my favourite crush drinks. It is a shining example of how to experiment with fruit combinations and inspiring for you to start experimenting with your own recipes. I use equal parts of both strawberries and mandarins, but you can use as much or as little as you like.

Makes 1 drink
3 large strawberries
½ mandarin, chopped and skins left on
2 teaspoons sugar
20ml / ¾oz sugar syrup (see p 25)
ice
45ml / ¾oz seriously ... pinky vodka

Crush and then shake with ice. Pour into your glass.

brekky and brunch crush drinks

Daytime crush drinks can be a very special part of any social gathering and particularly popular for brunch. They are easy to whip up and a great way to use up leftover fruit.

The sugar brings out the intense flavours and the addition of juices, yoghurt or champagne makes the drink brilliantly refreshing. Here's one of my favourites, Fruitonic: white peach, lime, ginger and sugar and sugar syrup, crushed then shaken with ice and finished off with Piper Heidsieck champagne.

Now here are some more refreshing crushers...

delicious fruitonic

dynamite

As the name suggests, the flavour is great and as my dad says, "That's dynamite!" Strawberry and mint just seem to be one of those rarely touched flavour combinations that has yet to find its way into most people's mouths. Don't worry if you don't have all the ingredients - just think of what else would work well and give it a shot.

Makes 1 drink

3 strawberries, pruned, washed and chopped

5 mint leaves, ripped

2 teaspoons caster sugar

20ml / ¾oz sugar syrup (see p 25)

ice

60ml / 2oz Ocean Spray Cranberry Classic juice

dash grenadine, optional

Crush and then shake with ice. Pour into your glass and garnish with a whole strawberry.

happy kiwi

This is a real kids' favourite. I never thought kids were that interested in yoghurt, but when they can make the drink themselves it's a whole different story.

Makes 1 drink

1½ kiwi fruits, peeled and chopped

3 teaspoons caster sugar

20ml / ¾oz sugar syrup (see p 25)

ice

60ml / 2oz yoghurt

½ passionfruit

Crush and then shake with ice. Pour into your glass and top with passionfruit pulp. Garnish with a kiwi fruit wheel.

move juice

This drink will keep you on your toes and buzzing around.

Makes 1 drink

½ glass chopped watermelon and pitted cherries

2 teaspoons caster sugar

20ml / ¾oz sugar syrup (see p 25)

ice

20ml / ¾oz orange juice

60ml / 2oz Ocean Spray Cranberry Classic juice

Crush and then shake with ice. Pour into your glass and garnish with
a cherry.

vitalizer

This recipe is just too easy because it uses two of the most popular
fruits around, pineapple and oranges.

*Cranberry juice goes extremely well with the sweetness
of these two fruits - all that natural sugar!*

Makes 1 drink

½ glass fresh pineapple and orange, chopped

2 teaspoons caster sugar

20ml / ¾oz sugar syrup (see p 25)

ice

60ml / 2oz Ocean Spray Ruby Red Grapefruit juice

½ pomegranate or a dash of grenadine

Crush and then shake with ice. Pour into your glass and garnish with
a slice of star fruit.

granita style crush drinks

Traditionally granitas are fresh fruit and sugar crushed with champagne and then frozen to make a dessert. I personally prefer to serve them as a lighter alternative to the vodka crush drinks covered earlier in this chapter.

Just one tip before I launch into some of my favourite recipes: keep your champagne cold after the preparation of the all the cocktails, as there is nothing worse than drinking warm champagne when you have run out of fruit to make more drinks.

For a virgin style granita, just add soda water, sparkling grape juice or lemonade. This is a refreshing alternative with an instantly sobering effect.

utopia

This drink is so more-ish that you may well find yourself having to explain your condition. Keep in mind though, that while champagne doesn't make you drunk, just more charming and witty, it can change your perceptions... all too fast. So I suggest a good meal if you are exploring these for brunch.

Makes 1 drink
½ glass blueberries, raspberries and strawberries
2 teaspoons caster sugar
20ml / ¾oz Chambord
ice
Piper Heidsieck champagne, to top

Crush and then shake with ice. Pour into your glass and then top with Piper Heidsieck champagne.

seriously ... crushing

joy

This is delicious and a little like Yin Yang (see p 48), but in this case I found that raspberries went extremely well with mandarins and champagne.

Makes 1 drink

½ mandarin, skins left on

6 raspberries

2 teaspoons caster sugar

20ml / ¾oz sugar syrup (see p 25)

ice

Piper Heidsieck champagne, to top

Crush and then shake with ice. Pour into your glass and then top with Piper Heidsieck champagne.

morning glory

Citrus fruit and exotic passionfruit go so well together that I reckon you could bottle this and become filthy rich. There is something about the tartness of pink grapefruit and the natural sweetness of passionfruit that are best explained by simply tasting them. Though any kind of citrus fruit in combination with passionfruit works really well with this recipe.

Makes 1 drink

¼ pink grapefruit, chopped and skins left on

1 passionfruit, pulp

2 teaspoons caster sugar

20ml / ¾oz Chambord

ice

Piper Heidsieck champagne, to top

Crush and then shake with ice. Pour into your glass and then top with Piper Heidsieck champagne.

supersonic

A mate of mine, Mimo, from Alassio in Italy, e-mailed me a recipe with chopped ginger and limes. On tasting it, I had to agree that the combined flavours are supersonic. One thing I did find interesting was that a ginger flavoured drink could be successful in Italy, where it's an unpopular flavour and hard to find.

Makes 1 drink
¾ fresh lime, chopped
1 tablespoon fresh ginger root, chopped
2 teaspoons caster sugar
20ml / ¾ oz sugar syrup (see p 25)
ice
Piper Heidsieck champagne, to top

Crush and then shake with ice. Pour into your glass and then top with Piper Heidsieck champagne.

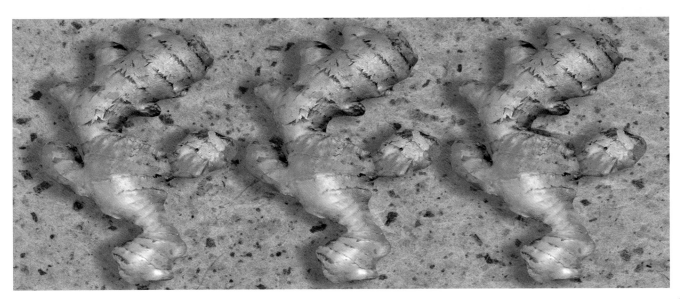

fresh ginger

crush drink food suggestions - by longrain restaurant and bar

peanut curry of duck with snake beans, chilli and sweet basil

grilled tuna with cucumber, mint and coriander and a roast eschallot dressing

caramelized pork hock with five spice and chilli vinegar

long and short drinks

As chairman of the Gin Appreciation Society in my hometown of Napier, New Zealand, I learned to appreciate the delicate but profound subtleties of long and short drinks. The society would meet once a week on Wednesdays and consisted of Nick, Blair, me and a bottle of gin.

We set ourselves the taxing task of consuming gin in various ways - we fondly referred to these occasions as GAS night. And although we all shared a common palate for cocktails and fish 'n' chips throughout the evening, we always understood the importance of keeping them in just that order.

One drink I have continued to have great success with since the days of GAS is the simple Gin and Tonic. Although many prefer a lemon wedge as the traditional garnish, I have added fruits and herbs like basil and blueberries, mint and lime or even rose water and grapefruit. The G & T will never be the same again.

To give you the long and the short of it all,
the difference between long and short drinks isn't
much more than artistic licence by the creator.

However, in my experience, to make the drink in a tall Highball, Collins, Old Fashioned or Rocks glass does have some result with the flavour and the presentation. In fact, it can very well be the difference between the drink going multi-platinum like the Cosmopolitan, or dying a sad lonesome death in the scribbles of someone's notebook.

In this chapter I show you how easy it is to build drinks. If you've never made cocktails before then this is a very good place to start.

tokyo do jo, watermelon cooler

long drinks

Think of long drinks as anytime drinks. Generally, long drinks have less alcohol content than short drinks and are much easier to drink so they tend to relax guests and warm them up for more to come later.

basic method - build

Fill the glass with ice and add the ingredients in the listed order (usually alcohol first). Garnish and serve.

Very simple, very easy, very cool.

sea breeze

Makes 1 drink

60ml / 2oz seriously ... vodka

60ml / 2oz Ocean Spray Cranberry Classic juice

30ml / 1oz Ocean Spray Ruby Red Grapefruit juice, to float

Build in a tall highball over ice and garnish with a citrus wedge.

From the famous Sea Breeze of Boston Massachusetts, I have made some great variations that follow.

street breeze

Makes 1 drink

60ml / 2oz seriously ... vodka

60ml / 2oz apple juice

30ml / 1oz ginger ale

ice

Build over ice in a tall highball glass and garnish with an apple slice.

lychee breeze

This is a great version of the classic. Its exotic sweet taste comes from the lychee.

Makes 1 drink

60ml / 2oz seriously ... vodka

60ml / 2oz juice from a tin of lychees

30ml / 1oz Ocean Spray Ruby Red Grapefruit juice

ice

Build over ice in a tall highball glass and garnish with lime rind and a sliced rambutan.

tokyo do jo

Makes 1 drink

30ml / 1oz Thai Ginger Bang Bang (see p 102)

30ml / 1oz sake

60ml / 2oz jasmine tea, unsweetened, steeped and chilled (see p 158)

30ml / 1oz soda water

ice

Build over ice in a tall highball glass and garnish with jasmine flowers. Be sure to wash your jasmine flowers or it might not be only yourself having a sip of this delicious drink.

icelandic iced tea, turkish iced tea, apricot tease, lychee breeze

icelandic iced tea

A variation on the Long Island Iced Tea which consists of: 15ml/½oz of each of the following: vodka, gin, light rum, Cointreau and sweet 'n' sour mix, topped with Coca Cola.

Makes 1 drink

15ml / ½oz seriously ... vodka

15ml / ½oz *ima*gin ... gin

15ml / ½oz Havana Club Silver dry rum

15ml / ½oz Cointreau

30ml / 1oz sweet 'n' sour (see p 25)

60ml / 2oz peppermint tea, sweetened, steeped and chilled (see p 158)

ice

Build over ice in a tall highball glass. Garnish with fresh mint leaves.

turkish iced tea

Makes 1 drink

30ml / 1oz seriously ... pinky vodka

30ml / 1oz Cointreau

30ml / 1oz Ocean Spray Cranberry Classic juice

5ml / 1 dash rosewater

60ml / 2oz fruit tea, sweetened, steeped and chilled (see p 158)

ice

Build over ice in a tall highball glass. Garnish with a sugar coated lemon rind.

apricot tease

Makes 1 drink

60ml / 2oz Hennessy V.S cognac

60ml / 2oz apricot nectar

30ml / 1oz Ocean Spray Ruby Red Grapefruit juice

ice

Build over ice in a tall highball glass. Garnish with orange rind.

white peach and mint julep

You could put this drink on the cusp of a crush and a long drink. In fact being both makes it versatile and very delicious.

Makes 1 drink
60ml / 2oz Maker's Mark bourbon
2 teaspoons caster sugar
20ml / ¾oz sugar syrup (see p 25)
½ fresh white peach, sliced thinly
8 mint leaves, large
60ml / 2oz soda water
crushed ice

Muddle the mint and a quarter of a peach in the base of a tall highball glass with caster sugar and sugar syrup. Then stir in the bourbon and pack the glass full of crushed ice. Add soda water and garnish with the remaining finely sliced peach.

the good old piña colada

As simple as it may be, there's no better way to make this drink. Dashes of coconut and pours of pineapple straight into a glass simply create an inconsistent drink. All you have to do is add rum to your Piña Colada mix and you're chilling out in style.

Makes 1 drink
60ml / 2oz Havana Club Añejo Reserva rum
120ml / 4oz Piña Colada mix (see p 27)
ice

Build over ice in a tall highball glass. Garnish with pineapple leaves and a coconut rim (see p 207).

bloody mary

There is nothing quite like a mix of vodka, tomato juice and spices to get your heart pumping.

My brother-in-law, Mark, is an avid fan of the Bloody Mary and taught me my appreciation of this old classic drink. The tradition he brought from Boston to the family is Bloody Marys on Christmas morning. This has never stopped us exercising the custom when we all get together over weekends at his place... it's an institution.

In the beginning of the book I showed you how to make Bloody, Thai and Wasabi Mary mix (see p 26). These simple mixers allow you to make the basis of your drink all in one go. Then it's a simple case of building the bloody things - quick as that!

bloody mary, bloody thai mary, bloody wasabi mary

A variation on the good old classic is to use one of the mixers listed in the mixers and garnish chapter near the front of this book.

Makes 1 drink
30ml / 1oz seriously ... vodka
120ml / 4oz Bloody Mary mix of your choice (see pp 26-27)
ice

Build over ice in a tall highball and garnish with lemongrass slithers.

short drinks

It's been said that the Old Fashioned cocktail died with the introduction of trashy 80's styled drinks of blue and green. Today drinks have become more sophisticated now that people are becoming more selective with drinking. Personally, I like to think of short drinks as very mature and hip.

old fashioned

It's hard to find a bar that makes a good Old Fashioned cocktail so if you are particular about the way you like it, this is a good starting point.

I don't use a maraschino cherry in my old fashioned as the flavour reminds me of a bad birthday party that had too many maraschino cherries and not enough bourbon.

If you're going to make a proper Old Fashioned
you'll need a little time up your sleeve. The process is by no means fast
but remember all great things take time.

Makes 1 Drink
90ml / 3oz Maker's Mark bourbon
3-4 teaspoons caster sugar
3-4 dashes Angostura Bitters
2 large orange rinds
ice

Use two large pieces of orange rind and twist one over the glass releasing citrus oils. Add Angostura Bitters and half the sugar plus a small amount of ice. Start to stir while bruising the orange, continually stirring the drink while adding more ice and Maker's Mark bourbon.

Once the glass contains diluted bourbon and orange flavours, twist the remaining orange rind over the top of the glass to release more flavours.

negroni

Thanks to Galliano sponsoring three of my tours to Italy that I learned to truly appreciate this legendary drink. It was at the end of my first tour that my agent, René Buléé, took my wife, Esmeralda, and I to a small aperitif bar in Como, in northern Italy, owned by Marco Violin. It was there that I sunk my first glass of the magic potion they call the Negroni. Coincidentally the place was called Gran Café Forever . . . Go Gran! (gran in Italian means grand or big).

Makes 1 drink
20ml / ¾oz *ima*gin ... gin
20ml / ¾oz Campari
20ml/ ¾oz sweet vermouth
orange rind
ice
soda water, optional to top

Build over ice in an old fashioned glass. Before garnishing, twist an orange rind to give the drink added orange flavour and aroma.

disco

This is a great drink Esmeralda invented one hot night in summer. Mango infused vodka with a chocolate disc to nibble on is as decadent as they come.

Makes 1 drink
45ml / 1½oz Mangocello - mango infused vodka (see p 95)
15ml / ½oz Chambord
90ml / 3oz Ocean Spray Cranberry Classic juice
ice

Shake all the ingredients in an ice filled shaker then pour over ice in a short glass.
Garnish with a chocolate disc (see p 36).

woody gets old fashioned

peachy rose gimlet

My beautiful wife Esmeralda came to me with this drink one night while we were having friends over for a gin party. The party involves each person mixing a round of drinks containing gin. To this day I don't think I could match the flavour and enjoyment with any other fruit combination. This cocktail has since then appeared on many of our event menus.

Makes 1 drink
60ml / 2oz *ima*gin ... gin
60ml / 2oz sweet 'n' sour (see p 25)
30ml / 1oz Peachy Rose mix (see p 31)
ice

Use an Old Fashioned glass and fill with ice and all the ingredients. Either stir well or shake by sealing a cocktail can over the rim of the glass. Garnish with a freshly squeezed lime wedge.

new york cosmopolitan

Our good friend Rob Cooper, from Chambord, believes this to be the original Cosmopolitan. Truly an icon of the Big Apple, the Cosmopolitan is finally firmly etched in my mind as a modern day classic cocktail.

Makes 1 drink
45ml / 1½oz seriously ... vodka
15ml / ½oz Chambord
30ml / 1oz sweet 'n' sour (see p 25)
60ml / 2oz Ocean Spray Cranberry Classic juice
dash egg white (see p 2045)
ice

Shake all the ingredients in an ice filled shaker and pour over ice in a cocktail glass. Garnish with a lime wedge.

sahara

Combining the ingredients in this drink are so delicious you just can't go wrong with the flavour. A real crowd pleaser.

Makes 1 drink
30ml / 1oz sweetened strawberry purée
60ml / 2oz Havana Club Añejo Reserva rum
60ml / 2oz mango nectar
30ml / 1oz passionfruit pulp
ice

stage 1 - sweetened strawberry purée

Makes 500ml / 16½oz of purée, or approximately 16 drinks
350g / 11½oz fresh strawberries
1 cup cold water
1 cup brown sugar

Prune and wash two punnets of strawberries. Blend the ingredients thoroughly with one cup of brown sugar and one cup of water. Transfer to a jug or container.

stage 2 - build

Build the ingredients over an ice packed glass in the listed order to give a coloured layered effect.

watermelon cooler

Makes 1 drink
45ml / 1½oz Jose Cuervo tequila
15ml / ½oz Cointreau
60ml / 2oz watermelon juice, sweetened
30ml / 1oz Ocean Spray Ruby Red Grapefruit juice
ice

stage 1 - sweetened watermelon juice

Makes 1Lt / 33oz, or approximately 16 drinks
500g / 16½oz watermelon, chopped, preferably seedless
1 cup cold water
1 cup caster sugar

Pack a blender with chunks of fresh de-skinned watermelon. Add one cup of caster sugar and one cup of water. Blend the ingredients thoroughly and transfer to a jug or container.

If you're not happy with the texture, strain the broken seeds through a strainer, using a spoon to help move the pulp aside.

stage 2 - build

Build the ingredients over an ice packed glass in the listed order. Garnish with fresh mint leaves.

long and short drink food suggestions - by bayswater brasserie

king salmon thinly sliced and topped with cucumber, chives, chervil, radicchio, lime segments and salmon roe

duck and pork braised with garlic and thyme on an onion jam filled pastry shell with sliced figs

rock and angasi oysters with an eschallot vinegar dressing

diydiydiydiydiydiy**diydiydiydiy**

diydiydiydiydiydiy**diydiydiydiy**

d.i.y liqueurs

When I was 14 years old my mum and dad went on a week's holiday to Melbourne and left my two older brothers and I to fend for ourselves. Bored and mischievous I set myself the challenge of making alcohol.

I found an empty 20 gallon drum that my dad used for storing maize to feed the animals on the farm and filled it with sugar water. I then wrapped fruits, starch vegetables, grains, nuts, seeds and pretty much anything else I could get my hands on in mutton cloth and submerged them in the barrel. I left the brew hidden in the loft with a sachet of yeast on top which just proved I really didn't have a clue what I was doing.

After about six months I thought I should check on my experiment. Emerging from the broth was a giant grey fungus, which I'm sure, could breath of its own accord. After removing the fungus, I siphoned this smelly concoction into 16 wine bottles and secretly stored them around the back of the shed.

After leaving the now doubling in alcohol stage of the experiment for a further three months, one weekend I discovered when I could get really silly and perform a crude M*A*S*H style distillation. Using an old kettle I attached an old piece of hose to the spout. What I believed to be higher-grade alcohol was produced by heating the fermented ingredients to evaporate and then condense in the pipe; dripping into a bowl on the floor. The final result - jazzed up with a sickening addition of spirits from my dad's liquor cabinet - was named The Eagle Rock Experience and was a potentially poisonous mixture of 89% proof wood alcohol.

Despite my shaky start, be assured that these listed recipes dictate a more palatable selection of 'do it yourself' liqueurs.

basic recipe

Depending on the recipe, you usually need a selection of spirits, fresh fruits and maybe a spice or two. Sugar is a common ingredient in this chapter and cream also features strongly. It's very easy to improvise with these recipes so if you are missing any of the ingredients, use your imagination to create your own liqueur.

A good way to make any d.i.y. liqueur stretch further
is to pour them up in smaller bottles such as dessert wine bottles.

basic method - infuse

Prepare your fruit and ingredients, leaving the skins on citrus. Place your ingredients in a large pot and warm over the stove on a low temperature with half the alcohol required. Continually stir the ingredients while over the heat for 20 minutes. Do not boil.

Once removed from the heat, add the remaining half of the alcohol for the infusion to continue. Leave the infusion covered in a cool place for 24-48 hours and mix all the flavours thoroughly every six hours. Strain the liqueur into clean bottles and soak corks before sealing. This will help keep the liqueur for longer.

Where spices are required, dry roast these first before adding wet ingredients. Creamy liqueurs keep for up to three weeks in the fridge while infused non-creamy liqueurs should be drunk within eight weeks. A good tip is to write a best before date on the bottle.

basic ingredients

Makes 2 x 700ml / 23½oz bottles
1kg / 33oz fruit or ingredients
4 cups sugar
750ml / 25oz non-alcoholic ingredients eg. water or cream
700ml / 23½oz spirit eg. vodka, rum etc.

infusing lemons and vodka

lemoncello

My old mate Michele De Carlo from Italy gave me this recipe while we were in Sicily and Mt Etna was blowing her stack. The best Lemoncello comes from Sicily where the lemon trees are grown in the rich volcanic mineral soil. Lemoncello is traditionally drunk after a meal and is served very cold in a shot glass. It is mild in alcohol, normally below 22% alcohol by volume, so you can enjoy more than one without losing the plot.

Makes 2 x 700ml bottles / 47oz, or approximately 45 drinks
8 lemons, unpeeled and chopped into large chunks
2 lemons, rind only
4 large cups caster sugar
1 x 700ml / 23½oz seriously ... vodka
750ml / 25oz water

Place the lemons and sugar into a large pot and bruise the fruit. Add the alcohol and water to the pot and allow to infuse for 48 hours. Strain the fruit using a sieve and pour through a funnel into empty bottles. Serve well chilled.

A nice alternative for this recipe is to replace the lemons with mangoes (remove the skins), peaches, pears, tangerines or pink grapefruit.

lemon vanilla fizz

Makes 1 drink
1 vanilla pod
2 lemon or lime leaves, or lemon rind
60ml / 2oz Lemoncello
ice
soda water, to top

Muddle the lemon leaves and half the vanilla pod in with a dash of Lemoncello. Pack a glass with ice and add the remaining Lemoncello. Top with soda water. Garnish with the remaining vanilla pod.

lemoncello sorbette

This is a delightful drink that you give yourself once in a while for being so damn good at being yourself. Hey, you might even have one a day...

Makes 1 drink
45ml / 1½oz Lemoncello
1 scoop vanilla ice cream
60ml / 2oz Piper Heidsieck champagne, chilled

Put a scoop of ice cream and Lemoncello into a handled pint glass. Whisk with a fork until the mix is smooth in consistency. Continue beating the ingredients and slowly add the champagne until the mix grows into a frothy creamy white mass that fills the glass. Scoop and serve into a cocktail glass with spoon.

citrus drop

Makes 1 drink
30ml / 1oz Lemoncello
30ml / 1oz Cointreau
30ml / 1oz Ocean Spray Ruby Red Grapefruit juice
60ml / 2oz sweet 'n' sour mix (see p 25)
ice

Shake all the ingredients in an ice filled shaker and then strain into a small glass.
Extremely refreshing.

dakota liqueur

This creamy 'advocaat' type liqueur, which is native to the many Caribbean Islands of Dutch descent, has long been one of the exotic presents I like to give to my friends and family.

This is a little different to the basic method shown at the beginning of this chapter and it requires good preparation and timing so that the non-alcoholic ingredients don't turn to custard.

Makes 2 x 700ml bottles / 47oz, or approximately 45 drinks
3 cinnamon sticks
8 cardamom pods
3 teaspoons nutmeg, ground
10 cloves
8 egg yolks
250ml / 8½oz fresh cream
250ml / 8½oz fresh milk
4 cups caster sugar
1 x 700ml / 23½oz Havana Club Añejo Reserva rum

stage 1 - cream base

Separate the yolks and add to a mixing bowl with cream. Whisk until a smooth creamy mixture is achieved.

stage 2 - flavour component

Dry roast the cinnamon, cardamom, nutmeg and cloves on a high heat for one minute in a medium sized saucepan. Be sure not to burn as this will tarnish the flavour. Add half a cup of rum, two cups of sugar and lower the heat to simmer. Keep stirring the ingredients constantly for a further eight minutes and add a little more rum as the contents evaporate in order to keep the liquid level at approximately half a cup.

stage 3 - heating

Pour the whisked creamy mixture into a large pot over low heat and keep stirring while slowly adding in the remaining sugar and milk.

Remember to constantly move the mixture and never allow it to boil. Keep this up for approximately 15 minutes until the mixture begins to thicken and then remove from the heat.

stage 4 - combining

Combine the flavour component to the egg cream base by straining through a sieve. Be sure to stir the warm creamy mixture well. Allow it to cool and then bottle.

tony making dakota liqueur

dakota choc gold

Makes 1Lt / 33½oz, or approximately 10 drinks

180ml / 6oz Dakota liqueur

60ml / 2oz Galliano gold liqueur

2 ripe bananas

120ml / 4oz pineapple

120ml / 4oz half 'n' half (see p 25)

ice

60ml / 2oz chocolate topping

Add all the ingredients except the chocolate sauce before blending thoroughly. Pour the drink into chilled cocktail glasses and then garnish with a chocolate topping spider web (see p 36).

honey walnut crème liqueur

Makes 2 x 700ml bottles / 47oz, or approximately 45 drinks

15 walnuts, peeled and un-roasted

250gm / 8½oz honey

2 cups brown sugar

500ml / 17oz fresh cream

50ml / 1½oz fresh milk

1 x 700ml / 23½oz bottle Cointreau

Roast the walnuts in an oven on medium-high heat for 10 minutes. Add them to a pot with the brown sugar and half a bottle of Cointreau. Stir well for 10 minutes while simmering and then remove the walnuts with a slotted spoon.

Add honey, cream and milk and simmer for a further five minutes while continually stirring the ingredients. Remove from heat and then stir in the remaining Cointreau before allowing to cool and bottling. Serve over ice or pre-chilled.

honey walnut crème liqueur

raspberry honey nuts

Sometimes a strictly cream-based drink can be a bit too rich for some, and this is why the use of half cream to half milk, half 'n' half, is a very important ingredient as it makes the cocktail lighter and easier to drink.

Makes 1 drink

30ml / 1oz Honey Walnut Crème liqueur (see p 92)

30ml / 1oz Chambord

60ml / 2oz half 'n' half (see p 25)

ice

5 raspberries

Build on ice into a chilled cocktail glass. Garnish with fresh raspberries.

blair relaxes with raspberry honey nuts

imperial vodka

Makes 2 x 700ml bottles / 47oz, or approximately 45 drinks

2 limes or lemons, chopped

2 mandarins, chopped

2 bananas, chooped

4 cups caster sugar

700ml / 23½oz water

700ml / 23½oz seriously ... vodka

Use the basic infusion method for this delicious liqueur (see p 84). Serve chilled.

peach cognac

Makes 2 x 700ml bottles / 47oz, or approximately 45 drinks

5 peaches, chopped

4 cups caster sugar

700ml / 23½oz water

700ml / 23½oz Hennessy V.S cognac

Use the basic infusion method for this delicious liqueur (see p 84). Serve chilled.

mangocello

Makes 2 x 700ml bottles / 47oz, or approximately 45 drinks

4 mangoes, chopped

3 severed and split vanilla pods

4 cups caster sugar

700ml / 23½oz water

700ml / 23½oz seriously ... vodka

Use the basic infusion method for this delicious liqueur (see p 84). Serve chilled.

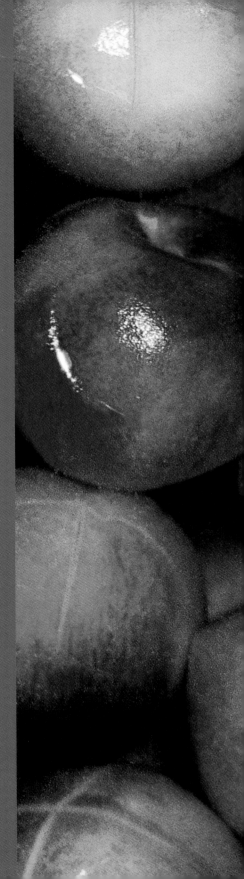

sloe gin

This is traditionally a straight infusion of sloe plums, sugar and good quality gin, such as *ima*gin ... gin. Normally one would leave the concoction until the pips separate from their skins and the sediment has settled before siphoning out the infusing liquid. But I sped the recipe up a little so you don't have to wait six to seven months to enjoy the fruits of your labour.

Makes 1 Lt / 33½oz, or approximately 10 drinks
30 red flesh plums
300g palm or plum sugar
300ml / 10oz water
400ml / 13½oz *ima*gin ... gin

Remove the skins from the plums by piercing their skins with a cross using a knife. Place in boiling water for one minute. Pour cold water over them and gently remove the skins leaving unblemished naked flesh. Fill a large empty juice bottle with whole plums.

Make a sugar syrup using the palm sugar and water (see p 25), and add to the bottle or jar of plums. Add the gin and shake thoroughly. Leave to infuse for three to four days before serving.

The longer you leave it the more flavoursome it becomes.

sloe sloppy joe

Makes 1 drink
20ml / ¾oz Sloe Gin
20ml / ¾oz espresso coffee
20ml / ¾oz cream whipped with a teaspoon of caster sugar

Pour the pre-chilled Sloe Gin into a large highball glass. Use a teaspoon to assist in layering the hot espresso coffee and then spoon on whipped cream. Garnish with ground cinnamon or nutmeg.

sloe gin fizz

This is a golden oldie and with the availability of commercial Sloe Gin becoming more scarce, this may very well be the drink that is both unique and satisfying at your next late night get together. It's a great welcome drink because of its refreshing nature and light fizz.

Makes 1 drink
60ml / 2oz Sloe Gin
30ml / 1oz of sweet 'n' sour mix (see p 25)
1 dash egg white (see p 205)
60ml / 2oz soda water
ice

Mix the ingredients excluding the soda water in a large ice filled cocktail shaker. Fill your glass with ice and then three quarters full with the mixture, then top with soda water and garnish with a lemon squeeze. Very simple and very tasty.

sloe soul elevator

This drink will elevate any gathering to some great conversation.

Makes 1 drink
¼ cup blueberries
20ml / ¾oz sugar syrup (see p 25)
30ml / 1oz Cointreau
40ml orange juice, freshly squeezed
30ml / 1oz Sloe Gin
ice

Place the blueberries in a large highball glass and leave some for garnish. Add the sugar syrup and muddle (see p 41). Pack glass with crushed ice and build drink (see p 64). Add Cointreau, orange juice and Sloe Gin in that order. Garnish with blueberries on top.

spicy mexican coffee liqueur

The beauty of this liqueur is that it is very smooth, yet has a little bang at the end. If you just love chilli then don't hold back for that big bang. This is a brilliant drink for cold winter gatherings.   Served hot or cold, it can provide even more depth to your cup of coffee.

Makes 2 x 700ml bottles / 47oz, or 45 approximately drinks
1-2 teaspoons dried chilli flakes or 1 teaspoon ground chilli
½ teaspoon cumin
500ml / 17oz espresso or freshly brewed coffee
300gm / 10oz good quality unsweetened cooking chocolate
4 cups brown sugar
1 x 700ml / 23½oz Jose Cuervo tequila

Grind the chilli and cumin with a pestle and mortar into a very fine powder. Then in a large saucepan over a medium heat stir in the brewed coffee and the ground spices. Add the cooking chocolate and sugar and stir until all the ingredients have dissolved. Once smooth in texture remove from the heat and add tequila. Allow it to cool, strain and then bottle.

spicy mexican affogato

I absolutely love affogatos. The decadent nature of this drink with its smooth creaminess, temperature change and sweet bitter taste combination all of a sudden stops me talking and starts me stirring and slurping very contentedly.

Makes 1 drink
30ml / 1oz Spicy Mexican Coffee liqueur
60ml / 2oz hot espresso coffee
1 large scoop vanilla ice cream

Place a neat scoop of ice cream in a small bowl and pour piping hot espresso and Spicy Mexican Coffee liqueur over the top. Use a spoon to devour this little treat.

kentucky berry liqueur

This is a sweet liqueur that is best served at the beginning of the night as an aperitif because of its hunger inducing character.

Makes 2 x 700ml bottles / 47oz, or approximately 45 drinks
700ml / 23½oz Maker's Mark bourbon
15ml / ½oz sugar syrup
800ml / 27oz water
1 punnet strawberries
1 punnet raspberries
4 cups caster sugar
ice

Dissolve the sugar in the water and then infuse all the ingredients in a bowl. Add Maker's Mark and let sit for 24-48 hours. Strain before bottling and chill berfore serving.

This liqueur is delicious served on ice with a dash of soda water. Garnish with fresh raspberries.

spicy mexican coffee liqueur

thai ginger bang bang

One of the trademarks of Thailand is Sang Som or Sang Tip Rum. Made from distilled fermented molasses, they're somehow infused with amphetamines and other mind-altering additions unique to Thailand. Only found in Thailand, these rums are for adventurous travellers and not for a quiet afternoon Caipiriñha.

In an attempt to emulate these concoctions, I have chosen Havana Club Añejo Reserva rum as the base alcohol because of its robust character and quality. This is a wonderful drink with soda water and a squeeze of lime, but can be a great chilled shot all on its own.

Sipping on one of these shots always results in a happy ending.

Makes 2 x 700ml bottles / 47oz, or approximately 45 drinks

1 cup fresh ginger, chopped

½ cup coconut, grated

1 lemongrass stem, chopped roughly

1 chilli, sliced

2 cups palm sugar

2 cups caster sugar

750ml / 25oz water

700ml / 23½oz Havana Club Añejo Reserva rum

4 lime leaves

Caramelize the ginger, coconut and lemongrass in a large saucepan with the palm sugar and a dash of water for eight minutes. Add half the bottle of rum, the remaining sugar, chilli and water to a saucepan and simmer for 15-20 minutes while continually stirring to dissolve the sugars.

Allow the brew to cool and sieve out the solids before adding the remaining rum. Bottle and keep in the fridge. Lasts approximately four weeks.

ginger caipiriñha

Makes 1 drink
1½ limes, chopped
2 teaspoons caster sugar
15ml / ½oz sugar syrup
30ml / 1oz Thai Ginger Bang Bang
30ml / 1oz Havana Club Añejo Reserva rum
ice

Put chopped limes, caster sugar and sugar syrup in a glass. Use a crush stick/French rolling pin to crush these ingredients down until you have a juicy mash. Fill the glass with ice, Thai Ginger Bang Bang and rum. Shake all the ingredients and pour.

thai-foon

Makes 1 drink
60ml / 2oz Thai Ginger Bang Bang (see p 102)
60ml / 2oz apple juice
60ml / 2oz ginger ale
ice

Fill the glass with ice and build using the ingredients in the listed order. Garnish with lemongrass slithers and serve.

Very exotic, very delicious.

d.i.y liqueurs food suggestions - by lyndey milan from her book 'fabulous food'

glass noodle salad with peanut and red onion

asian-style roast pork salad with fresh coriander

spiced quail with nam jim

dmksdmksdmksdmksdmks
dmksdmksdmksdmksdmks

d.m.k.s - daiquiris, margaritas, kamikazes and sidecars

I want to let you in on a little secret about my favourite drink. I call it a Mineken and to cut a long story short, it's a Margarita in one hand and a Heineken beer in the other. Some may think I am bordering on liquid psychosis, but it's really satisfying alternating between the two, plus it also saves me going back to the bar for at least an hour.

If you try my favourite drink, don't be afraid to try one of my special flavoured versions like a Caramelized Apple and Cinnamon Mineken...look out!

In this chapter you'll discover just how simple it is to make the basic drinks that make up the majority of cocktails consumed around the world. I'm not talking about complex recipes with hard-to-find ingredients. It's all about using base ingredients to make great tasting drinks and then adding your personal touch to make any dinner party a cracker.

peachy rose margarita and a vanilla tangerine sidecar

basic recipe

Being able to make good fresh sweet 'n' sour (see p 25) is a large part of making a good Margarita, Daiquiri, Kamikaze or a Sidecar. Using fresh lemons or limes in place of long-life products will inevitably be the difference between a mediocre and a really fantastic drink!

Summing up the subtle differences between these three often confused drinks, I have the following formula:

45ml / 1½oz base spirit
15ml / ½oz Cointreau
90ml / 3oz sweet 'n' sour mix
ice

basic ingredients

A Daiquiri uses rum as the base spirit and can have a sugar rim.
A Margarita uses tequila as the base spirit and can have a salt rim.
A Kamikaze uses vodka as the base spirit and can have a sugar rim.
A Sidecar uses cognac as the base spirit and can have a sugar rim.
For rimming method (see p 207).

basic method

If you would like to make a drink using a concentrated mixer, follow the recipe below:

Makes 1 drink
45ml / 1½oz base spirit
15ml / ½oz Cointreau
60ml / 2oz sweet 'n' sour mix (see p 25)
30ml / 1oz concentrated mix (see p 28)
ice

basic method

shaken - served up (without ice in the glass)

Pre-chill glass with ice. Add all the ingredients to an ice filled shaker and shake until thoroughly mixed. Remove the ice from chilled glass and pour your cocktail into a 150ml/5oz cocktail glass. A common optional ingredient in shaken drinks is a dash of egg white (see p 205), which gives the drink a light consistency and adds a fresh froth to the surface.

shaken - served on the rocks (with ice in the glass)

Pack 390ml/13oz highball glass with ice. Add all the ingredients to an ice filled shaker and shake until thoroughly mixed. Pour your cocktail from the cocktail shaker into a pre-prepared glass. Optional egg white (see p 205).

blended - served frozen (without ice in the glass)

A basic rule of thumb for making frozen drinks is:
the amount of cubed ice it takes to fill a glass
is the perfect amount of ice to use when blended with the listed ingredients.

Add 'rule of thumb' measured ice to a blender cup, then add the listed ingredients and blend until smooth. Four drinks per blender is usually the maximum. If the mix freezes in the base of the blender, stopping the surface of the ingredients from moving, remove the blender and give it a shake before blending again.

Getting blended drinks consistent in their density can take a little time, so don't be afraid to add a little more liquid to get it moving again.

Blending drinks without alcohol and loads of ice can be a bit tricky, as it's the alcohol that stops the mix from freezing up prematurely. My suggestion is to add sugar syrup to blended fruit drinks, as ingredients high in sugar freeze less than those with just a water base.

caramelized apple cinnamon margarita, quince mango kamik

caramelized apple cinnamon margarita

Makes 1 drink

45ml / 1½oz Jose Cuervo tequila

15ml / ½oz Cointreau

60ml / 2oz sweet 'n' sour mix (see p 25)

30ml / 1oz Caramelized Apple Cinnamon mix (see p 29)

ice

Blend all the ingredients with ice and serve. Garnish with a cinnamon stick and a lime wedge.

quince mango kamikaze

Makes 1 drink

45ml / 1½oz seriously ... vodka

15ml / ½oz Cointreau

60ml / 2oz sweet 'n' sour mix (see p 25)

30ml / 1oz Quince Mango mix (see p 29)

ice

Shake all the ingredients with ice and serve. Garnish with a sugar rim (see p 207) and a lime wheel.

vanilla tangerine sidecar

Makes 1 drink

45ml / 1½oz Hennessy V.S cognac

15ml / ½oz Cointreau

60ml / 2oz sweet 'n' sour mix (see p 25)

30ml / 1oz Vanilla Tangerine mix (see p 29)

ice

Shake all the ingredients with ice and serve. Garnish with an orange rind.

mango lychee sidecar

Makes 1 drink

45ml / 1½oz Hennessy V.S cognac

15ml / ½oz Cointreau

60ml / 2oz sweet 'n' sour mix (see p 25)

30ml / 1oz Mango Lychee mix (see p 30)

ice

Shake all the ingredients with ice and serve. Garnish with a rambutan half.

raspberry mint daiquiri

Makes 1 drink

45ml / 1½oz Havana Club Silver dry rum

15ml / ½oz Cointreau

60ml / 2oz sweet 'n' sour mix (see p 25)

30ml / 1oz Raspberry Mint mix (see p 30)

ice

Shake all the ingredients with ice and serve. Garnish with fresh mint and raspberries.

pineapple mint margarita

Makes 1 drink

45ml / 1½oz Jose Cuervo tequila

15ml / ½oz Cointreau

60ml / 2oz sweet 'n' sour mix (see p 25)

30ml / 1oz Pineapple Mint mix (see p 30)

ice

Blend all the ingredients with ice and serve. Garnish with a salt rimmed glass (see pg 207) and a lime wedge.

lychee lemongrass kamikaze

Makes 1 drink

45ml / 1½oz seriously ... vodka

15ml / ½oz Cointreau

60ml / 2oz sweet 'n' sour mix (see p 25)

30ml / 1oz Lychee Lemongrass mix (see p 31)

ice

Shake all the ingredients with ice, strain and serve. Garnish with lemongrass slithers.

raspberry plum sidecar

Makes 1 drink

45ml / 1½oz Hennessy V.S cognac

15ml / ½oz Cointreau

60ml / 2oz sweet 'n' sour mix (see p 25)

30ml / 1oz Raspberry Plum mix (see p 31)

ice

Blend all the ingredients with ice and serve. Garnish with fresh raspberries.

peachy rose margarita

Makes 1 drink

45ml / 1½oz Jose Cuervo tequila

15ml / ½oz Cointreau

60ml / 2oz sweet 'n' sour mix (see p 25)

30ml / 1oz Peachy Rose mix (see p 31)

ice

Shake all the ingredients with ice and serve. Garnish with pink rose petals.

raspberry plum sidecar

d.m.k.s drinks food suggestions - by katering caterers

vegetarian quesadillas with salsa, sour cream and guacamole

salmon ballontine with lime aioli on a crisp potato roesti

steamed Peking duck crepes with shallots and hoisin sauce

mmmmmmmmmmmmmmmmm

mmmmmmmmmmmmmmmmmmm

martinis

I used to shake my head as vigorously as a Boston shaker as the sight of a Martini. Nowadays, they're very modish, having befriended many a drinker in their time. But up until a few years ago, my friends and I would've avoided the insidious idea of drinking so much hard alcohol. Then I started to really appreciate the beauty of chilled flavoured alcohol... and the glasses got smaller.

basic recipe

The most commonly confusing element of making a Martini is the amount of vermouth to use.

In short, the less dry vermouth used implies a dryer Martini, and the more dry vermouth used denotes this as a more classic Martini, which is the less popular of the two variations these days.

Makes 1 drink
60ml / 2oz gin or vodka
2-3 drops of dry vermouth
2 queen size olives speared on a toothpick

Variations on the classic martini include the Gibson, which includes rubbing half a garlic clove around the inside of the chilled glass before serving and using cocktail onions in place of olives as the garnish. The Buckeye Martini uses a pitted Kalamata olive in place of a green Spanish one but requires 15ml/½oz of vermouth. It's all a bit daunting really, so I suggest you work to the above recipe if you're making a standard Martini.

In this chapter I have a great selection of modern Martini styled drinks that are sure to get your tastebuds jumping!

jasmine and vanilla martini

basic method - stir

Chill your glasses with ice first. Combine the entire ingredients in an ice filled shaker and stir the ingredients with a long spoon 8-10 times. Remove the ice from chilled glasses. Strain the ingredients from the shaker into chilled glasses.

french martini

Makes 1 drink

45ml / 1½oz seriously ... vodka

15ml / 1½oz Chambord

60ml / 2oz pineapple juice

ice

Shake vigorously with ice and strain the ingredients into a small martini glass. Delicious.

martini mandarin

Makes 1 drink

45ml / 1½oz seriously ... vodka

10ml / ¼oz Cointreau

30ml / 1oz mandarin juice

30ml / 1oz sugar syrup (see p 25)

ice

Stir with ice and strain the ingredients into chilled glass. Garnish with mandarin rind.

french martini with chambord

jasmine and vanilla martini

Makes 1 drink

50ml / 1¾oz seriously ... vodka

30ml / 1oz jasmine tea, unsweetened, steeped and chilled (see p 158)

2 teaspoons caster sugar

½ vanilla pod, severed and split

ice

Stir with ice and strain ingredients from shaker into chilled glass. Garnish with a split vanilla pod.

lychee lemongrass martini

Makes 1 drink

60ml / 2oz seriously ... vodka

30ml / 1oz Lychee Lemongrass mix (see p 31)

1 lemon wedge (see p 35), squeezed

ice

Stir with ice and strain ingredients from shaker into chilled glass. Garnish with sizeable strips of lemongrass.

easy chocolate martini

This Martini is the epitome of "ooh la la" in a drink.

Makes 1 drink

50ml / 1¾ oz seriously ... vodka

30ml / 1oz white crème de cacao

ice

Stir with ice and strain the ingredients from shaker into chilled glass. Garnish with a chocolate disc (see p 36) .

martini mandarin, easy chocolate martini

tabletop tequini

Makes 1 drink

60ml / 2oz Jose Cuervo tequila

30ml / 1oz green seedless grape juice (blending with sugar and sieving table grapes)

2 teaspoons caster sugar

ice

Stir with ice and strain the ingredients from the shaker into chilled glass. Garnish with speared grapes.

peppermint tini

Makes 1 drink

50ml / 1¾ oz seriously ... vodka

30ml / 1oz peppermint tea, unsweetened, steeped and chilled (see p 158)

2 teaspoons caster sugar

1 mint lolly

ice

Stir with ice and strain the ingredients into a small martini glass. Garnish with a mint leaf and lolly.

cranberry martini

Makes 1 drink

60ml / 2oz seriously ... pinky vodka

30ml / 1oz Ocean Spray Cranberry Classic juice

½ teaspoon caster sugar

1 lime wedge, squeezed

ice

Stir with ice and strain the ingredients from the shaker into chilled martini glass. Garnish with speared blueberries.

kiwi tequini

Makes 1 drink
60ml / 2oz Jose Cuervo tequila
30ml / 1oz sugar syrup (see p 25)
1 kiwi fruit, peeled and diced
ice

Muddle the kiwi fruit in the base of the cocktail shaker with the sugar syrup. Add Jose Cuervo tequila then shake with ice and strain into a small martini glass. Garnish with a kiwi fruit wheel.

plum tequini

Muddling brings out great flavours in fruits and this is just another way of exploring this method.

Making fruit Martinis like this opens infinite exploration of flavours and combinations, so don't be afraid to give it a go with anything from your fruit bowl!

Makes 1 drink
60ml / 2oz Jose Cuervo tequila
30ml / 1oz sugar syrup (see p 25)
1 dark red plum
ice

Muddle the plum in the base of the cocktail shaker with the sugar syrup. Add Jose Cuervo tequila then stir with ice and strain into a small martini glass. Garnish with a curled lemon rind.

leonie enjoys a plum tequini

mango coconut tequini

Tequinis like this are so easy to slide down they slip you into another dimension. The mango and coconut flavour combination goes extremely well with a really smooth tequila, such as Jose Cuervo. Enjoy.

Makes 1 drink
60ml / 2oz Jose Cuervo tequila
2 drops coconut essence
30ml / 1oz sugar syrup (see p 25)
¼ large mango chopped, skins left on
ice

Muddle the mango pieces in the base of the cocktail shaker with the sugar syrup. Add Jose Cuervo tequila and the coconut essence. Shake with ice and strain the ingredients into a small chilled martini glass. Garnish with a coconut rim (see p 207).

jaffa tini

Makes 1 drink
30ml / 1oz Cointreau
30ml / 1oz white crème de cacao
15ml / ½oz orange juice
15ml / ½oz grenadine
ice

Combine entire ingredients in an ice filled shaker. Stir the ingredients with a long spoon 8-10 times. Strain the ingredients from the shaker into chilled martini glass. Garnish with a chocolate flake rim (see p 207) and orange rind (see p 34).

mango coconut tequini

martini food suggestions - by cherry bim

mini anti pasto veg stacks with pesto drizzle

chargrilled chicken breast fillet with lemon and rosemary

spinach and ricotta crepe with tomato tapenade

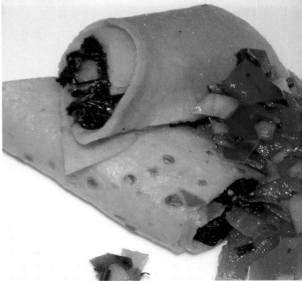

pppppppppppppppppppppppp
pppppppppppppppppppppppp

punches

When I left home at sixteen and moved to Wellington, New Zealand, my newfound flatmates introduced me to the cleansing Wringer washing machine punch. We would pour what ever turned up into that old washing machine which was constantly thrashing a brew around. Whenever you wanted a drink, all you had to do was to turn the machine onto spin cycle and out came a laughable serving of 'château de wringer'. Mmmm. Very cleansing. Maybe not?

Anyway, if you have a bunch of friends and family coming around in five minutes and they're expecting miracles out of you and your kitchen... relax.

Focus on the mighty punch.
It's easy and quick to make and
the most brilliant thing of all is that it's self service.

In this chapter I've included a few hot punches... to warm up your mind, body and soul... and hands in winter. The recipes have been adapted so that you can make them more quickly, with fewer complications.

All you need is a large bowl, jug or pot to mix and serve into glasses or cups.

mum's good old slap it together punch

mum's good old slap it together punch

This is a good family punch because it doesn't include alcohol.

Makes 5Lt / 166oz, or approximately 30 drinks
1 mint bunch
2Lt / 66½oz orange juice
1 packet jelly babies
1 punnet berries (your choice)
2-3 citrus fruits (your choice), sliced into wheels
½ cup lemon or lime juice
1Lt / 33½oz black tea, steeped, sweetened and chilled (see p 158)
1Lt / 33½oz lemonade
1Lt / 33½oz ginger ale
ice

Add all the ingredients to a punch bowl except the lemonade and ginger ale. Make sure to add the fizzies as guests arrive so the punch doesn't go flat.

pink planter's punch

Planters punch is the native punch of Jamaica. It is probably one of the best known punches of all. A good variation is to add Ocean Spray Ruby Red Grapefruit juice. This punch is a great party starter!

Makes 2Lt / 66½oz, or approximately 13 drinks
150ml / 5oz lime juice
3 cups caster sugar
1Lt / 33½oz Ocean Spray Ruby Red Grapefruit juice
350ml / 11½oz Havana Club Añejo Reserva rum
ice

Stir all the ingredients in large bowl until the sugar has dissolved. Garnish your punch with ruby red grapefruit wheels and serve in punch cups.

pink planter's punch

piper fruit

My good friend Antoine came to me some years ago with the idea of making his champagne fruitier. So, after endless trials and tribulations, experimenting with liqueurs and juices, came the fruity discovery of Piper Fruit. A simple yet superb drink. Enjoy it with a group of friends.

Makes 700ml / 23½oz, or approximately 5 drinks
350g / 11½oz seasonal stone fruit (your choice), sliced
350g / 11½oz berries (your choice)
200g / 6½oz caster sugar
700ml / 23½oz Piper Heidsieck champagne, chilled

Chop all your fruit and macerate with the sugar in a large jug for about 10 minutes. This allows the richness of the fruit to intensify. Pour half the bottle of chilled Piper over the fruit and leave the remaining half bottle on ice. Stir the fruit, sugar and champagne before half filling your cocktail glasses with the mix. Top up with the remaining chilled Piper before drinking.

stomping jungle punch

Please be forewarned about this drink. It is just one of those recipes that will send people crazy and tip the scales if too much is drunk without regular glasses of water. As the name suggests... it's wild!

Makes 5Lt / 166oz, or approximately 30 drinks
700ml / 23½oz Piper Heidsieck champagne
700ml / 23½oz seriously ... vodka
600ml / 20oz sugar syrup (see p 25)
500g / 16½oz fresh seasonal fruit (your choice), chopped
2Lt / 66½oz pineapple juice
ice

Mix all the ingredients in a large bowl and serve with ice.

picnic punch

This is a great idea if you feel like taking something different to a picnic in the park. Grab an empty juice bottle, thermos or flask that holds approximately 1Lt/33½oz of liquid. It can double as a shaker.

Makes 1Lt / 33½oz, or approximately 6½ drinks
200ml / 6½oz Jose Cuervo tequila
100ml / 3½oz Chambord
300ml / 10oz fruit purèe (see pg 22)
100ml / 3½oz mango nectar
200ml / 7oz fruit tea, steeped, sweetened and chilled (see p 158)
1 lime, juiced
ice

Add all the ingredients to a bottle and chill in a fridge or on ice. Shake and serve either on ice or if ingredients are cold enough, serve without ice as you like.

paradiso punch

Makes 5Lt / 166oz, or approximately 30 drinks

350ml / 11½oz Havana Club Silver dry rum

350ml / 11½oz Cointreau

1½Lt / 50oz Ocean Spray Ruby Red Grapefruit juice

1½Lt / 50oz Ocean Spray Cranberry Classic juice

60ml / 2oz sugar syrup (see p 25)

1 lime, juiced

500g favourite fresh fruits

ice

Mix all the liquid ingredients together in a large jug. Dice the fruit and stir through. Serve chilled.

sangria

The vivid memories of eating Tapas and drinking jugs of Sangria with Esmeralda in the small bars deep in the winding streets of Seville, will stay with me forever. The rich culture and flamboyant flamenco dancers have left me with a lasting impression that I revisit every time I make a jug of Sangria.

The secret to making good Sangria is not to make it too sweet or dry,
but somewhere in between so that it's so smooth
that you can hardly discern the alcohol and it just slides down.

Makes 2Lt / 66½oz, or approximately 13 drinks
700ml / 23½oz red wine
300ml / 10oz sugar syrup (see p 25)
500ml / 16½oz apple juice
300ml / 10oz Havana Club Añejo Reserva rum
90ml / 3oz Cointreau
2 limes, juiced
2 cinnamon sticks
1 blood orange, finely chopped
ice

Mix all the ingredients in a large jug and stir with a long wooden spoon. Be sure to keep the fruit in the mixture.

Serve chilled in wine glasses.

glögg

Even though this is typically known as the national drink of Sweden, I first drank this in Denmark on New Year's Eve years ago with some friends. The snow was piling up outside and it must have been 40° below zero, but really who cared? After two cups of this magic, I was walking on frozen water…. but that's another story.

Makes 2Lt / 66½oz, or approximately 13 drinks
1½Lt / 50oz red wine
500ml / 16½oz Hennessy V.S cognac
10 cloves
5 cardamom pods
2 cinnamon sticks
1 cup raisins or sultanas
½ cup almonds, chopped
2 cups brown sugar

Dry roast the almonds, cardamon pods, cloves and cinnamon sticks in a large pot for a minute on the stove on medium heat. Add the rest of the ingredients into the pot and stir. Simmer the brew for 10 minutes but do not boil. Just prior to serving, strain the ingredients.

If you like a bit of drama, ignite the surface of the Glögg, with extreme caution, and then sprinkle on a little brown sugar leaving it to caramelize for 10-15 seconds. Extinguish the flame by placing a lid over the pot to seal the air. Be sure you know exactly where the fire extinguisher is before you try this flaming trick! Alternately you can just serve it without all the show.

mario and belinda enjoy a glass of glögg

warm nectarine and pomegranate mulled wine

Makes 2Lt / 66½oz, or approximately 13 drinks

700ml / 23½oz white wine

150ml / 5oz Hennessy V.S cognac

1Lt / 33½oz water

4 cups sugar

5 nectarines, large and ripe

1 pomegranate

2 nutmegs, whole

orange rind

Place all the ingredients in a large pot. Simmer over medium heat for 10 minutes and strain before serving. Serve warm over the orange rind in large wine glasses or cups.

This delicious recipe can be made with peaches, plums, apples or figs.

cool apple and pear treat

Makes 2Lt / 66½oz, or approximately 13 drinks

600ml / 20oz apple juice

300ml / 10oz Hennessy V.S cognac

600ml / 20oz water

2 cups sugar

2 large pears, freshly peeled or tinned

1 lime, juiced

ice

Place the pears, sugar and water into a blender and purèe until smooth. Strain the blended ingredients through a strainer and pour into a bottle through a funnel. Add the lime juice, Hennessy V.S cognac and apple juice to the bottle and shake well before chilling in the fridge. Once chilled, be sure to reshake and serve on ice. Garnish with an apple slice.

lemon meringue punch

Makes 2Lt / 66½oz, or approximately 13 drinks

600g / 20oz lemon sorbet, good quality

500ml / 16½oz seriously ... vodka

6 large scoops vanilla ice cream, low fat

150ml / 5oz sugar syrup (see p 25)

ice

Soften the lemon sorbet in a microwave or in a dish with some hot water. In a large bowl whip the ice cream and the melted lemon sorbet together forming a nice and smooth mixture. While continually stirring add vodka and sugar syrup slowly.

Add some lime leaves to the punch for garnish and ladle into ice filled glasses.

150 punches

blushing rose punch

Makes 2Lt / 66½oz, or approximately 13 drinks

1Lt / 33½oz Ocean Spray Ruby Red Grapefruit juice

700ml / 23½oz seriously ... pinky vodka

300ml / 10oz sugar syrup (see p 25)

30ml / 1oz rosewater

700ml / 23½oz soda water

ice

Add all the ingredients to a bottle or jug and chill in the fridge. Serve either on ice or if ingredients are cold enough, serve without ice, as you like. Add the soda water just prior to serving and some pink rose petals for garnish.

sloe apricot soother

Makes 2Lt / 66½oz, or approximately 13 drinks

700ml / 23½oz apricot nectar

500ml / 16½oz seriously ... vodka

1 cup caster sugar

150ml / 5oz Sloe Gin (see p 97)

1 mango, peeled and diced

lime wheels

ice

soda water to top

Add all the ingredients to a punch bowl and chill with ice. Top with soda water just prior to serving.

punches food suggestions - by sabor de españa

tortilla de patatas - spanish style omelette made with onion and potato

albondigas con salsa de tomate - meatballs served in spicy tomato sauce

pulpo al la plancha - bbq baby octopus with alioli sauce

tttttttttttttttttttttttttttttttt
tttttttttttttttttttttttttttttttt

tea

My gran was the greatest traditional tea party planner I have ever known. Deep inside the china cabinet was stored a magnificent bone china tea set which I very gingerly had to remove and set for her afternoon tea parties.

I then performed the somewhat confusing task of taking orders and listening to old ladies go on about what they saw in the tea leaves. The presiding guests would turn the teapot this way and that, add sugar, milk, or lemon - all to perform the then very serious tea ceremony.

Tea has been around since time immemorial.

Going back centuries, broths of leafy herbs and roots were brewed to release their medicinal and healing properties. For those who suffer caffeine shakes from coffee, tea contains roughly a third to half the caffeine content of coffee.

In this chapter I give you an insight into the varieties available and the generously rewarding art of brewing tea.

basic method - brewing or steeping

Through the ages there has been a great deal said about the art of tea, therefore there is a bit to know about tea brewing. Firstly, tea needs exaggeratingly hot - or as hot as you can get - water to really bring out the true flavours that are held within.

Always preheat your teapot so it maintains its warmth with the brew using hot to boiling water. Empty the pot before refilling with hot water to steep your brew.

For the average person, a decent sized teapot will hold around 480ml/14-16oz of water, this should make four cups of tea and would entail four tea bags. The Brits believe tea should come in 24-26oz or just under 800ml pots, requiring four bags plus one more for the pot for good measure.

Turn the pot seven times clockwise to help steeping.
Steeping drastically improves your tea experience.

Always be sure to remove your tea bags if they contain black tea before serving, as leaving this type of tea in for too long will make the tea bitter.

basic ingredients

Some people think the difference between green, oolong and black tea refers to types of tea plants, but they simply refer to the method in which the tea is processed. Bearing this in mind, the brief descriptions of the differences are explained later in this chapter.

tea varieties

White tea, green tea, oolong tea, black tea, scented tea, fruit tea, compressed tea and medicinal tea.

white tea 'silver needles'

Prematurely picked buds that have a mild flavour and are very low in caffeine. They are dried and not fermented. Drink without milk.

green tea

Mature tea leaves that have a slightly bitter taste. They are usually steam dried. Drink without milk.

oolong tea 'chinese black dragon'

Slightly fermented leaves hold a distinctively pungent fruity flavour. Low in caffeine and smoother than black tea.

black tea 'tea-chest tea'

Fired so it produces a more bitter taste. Commonly found in tea bags, black tea is broken down into a finer grade to speed the steeping of the brew.

scented tea

Any tea variety mixed with the pleasant addition of floral ingredients like jasmine or rose or other varieties of bloomage.

fruit tea

Unique specialty teas including dried fruits and the occasional herb.

compressed tea

Incredibly cool and a major part of my interest in tea, are the bricks and blocks of compressed tea. Break off a chunk and brew it up.

root or medicinal tea

Roots, spices, fruits and herbs to create tonics for everything from sleep disorders to tummy aches and the common cold.

a great black tea brew

If you have the standard black tea in your pantry then here is a great way to begin your adventure into the world of the mighty brew.

Makes 1 x 480ml / 14-16oz teapot, or 4 drinks

2 tablespoons loose black tea, heaped or 4 tea bags

2 lemon or lime leaves, chopped or ½ lemon rinded

1 vanilla pod, scored with seeds

2 tablespoons honey

480ml / 14-16oz scolding hot water

In the customary way of western tea ceremonies, preheat your teacups. Layout saucers and teaspoons with a few good slices of teacake. Infuse all the ingredients for approximately 10 minutes before pouring.

Guests pay great attention to the tea ceremony and most people get quite excited when someone is confidently preparing a brew that is a little different to the norm.

rose and currant chillout tea

Makes 1 x 480ml / 14-16oz teapot, or 4 drinks

2 tablespoons loose white tea, heaped

½ cup currants and blueberries

2 rose buds, free of herbicides and sprays

2 tablespoons honey

480ml / 14-16oz scolding hot water

Infuse all the ingredients for approximately 10 minutes before pouring up to drink.

moroccan tea

I fell head over heels in love with this tea while I drove through Morocco. Because it's quite high in caffeine, toilet stops are frequent.

Traditionally the Moroccans are quite precise with their tea making and use large silver teapots, but for the purpose of trying this drink use whatever you have. It's the perfect way to enjoy mint in a hot drink.

Makes 1 x 480ml / 14-16oz teapot, or 4 drinks
2 tablespoons loose green tea, heaped
480ml / 14-16oz scolding hot water
fresh mint to fill 4 small glasses
sugar

Brew the tea in a teapot. Stuff your glasses full of mint leaves and if available orange blossoms for an authentic Morrocan tea experience. Roughly add one large tablespoon of sugar to each glass.

Once your brew has steeped enough,
pour from a comfortable height to give a frothy top to your tea.
Spills and splatters are all for authenticity.

Stir through the sugar and enjoy. Garnish with orange bloosoms.

potion tea

This recipe must pay homage to my soul mate Esmeralda, however I believe it has been around for about 500 years and she just calls it hers to save confusion. It's nothing short of a miracle tonic for sore throats and head colds and has even been known to help extinguish a full blown chesty flu and fever.

This potion is preferably drunk before going to bed and induces sweating to expel the flu from the body. To be perfectly blunt, it's not easy going, but trust me when I say that friends of ours have been full of praise and thanks for pushing them into trying this drink.

Makes 1 drink

1 small chilli, sliced in half

1 lemon wheel

1 teaspoon fresh ginger, chopped

2 tablespoon honey

1 lemon, juiced

1 pot oolong tea, brewed

Put all the ingredients in a plunger, except the lemon wheel. Let sit for five minutes before pouring. Garnish with a lemon wheel.

turkish delight tea

Makes 1 x 480ml / 14-16oz teapot, or 4 drinks

2 tablespoon loose green tea, heaped or 4 tea bags

4 turkish delight, generous sized pieces

1 tablespoon caster sugar

480ml / 14-16oz scolding hot water

Infuse all the ingredients for approximately five minutes before pouring up to drink.

plum blush tea

Makes 1 x 480ml / 14-16oz teapot, or 4 drinks

2 tablespoons loose chamomile tea, heaped or 4 tea bags

480ml / 14-16oz Ocean Spray Cranberry Classic juice

1 dark plum, sliced

1 rose bud

½ cup sugar

Steep the brew in cranberry juice for five minutes with the rose bud and the sliced plums. Stir in the sugar and strain before serving. Garnish with plum slices.

ginger iced tea

Makes 2Lt / 66½oz, or approximately 10 drinks

1 tablespoon loose black tea, heaped or 2 tea bags

500ml / 16½oz boiling hot water

2 tablespoon ginger, chopped

2 limes, juiced

2 cups caster sugar

1½Lt / 50oz of cold water

ice

Steep the tea and ginger in hot water for five minutes. Pour into a large jug or bottle and dissolve the sugar with the lime juice. Add the cold water and ice or leave in the fridge to cool before serving. For iced tea recipes using alcohol (see p 65-67).

classic usa style iced tea

My brother-in-law Mark, is from Boston, and he's an avid fan of this classic American icon. Normally it comes in dessicated tea sachets you can buy from any supermarket but in order to cut the cost of doing this, here is my recipe (that my brother-in-law refers to as 'the impostor').

Makes 2Lt / 66½oz, or approximately 10 drinks
1 tablespoon loose black tea, heaped or 2 tea bags
500ml / 16½oz of boiling hot water
1 tablespoon vanilla essence
2 lemons, juiced
2 cups caster sugar
1½Lt / 50oz of cold water
ice

Steep the tea in hot water for five minutes. Pour into a large jug or bottle and dissolve the sugar. Add the remaining ingredients and either top up with ice or leave in the fridge to cool before serving. As the name suggests, this tea must be served very cold.

chai tea - dry

As they say in India, "it's stronger than vodka, has more kick than rum and cheaper than whiskey". Chai Tea is the national drink of India. It is the catalyst for most social gatherings and I serve it at most meetings as a point of difference. The following recipe will be enough to make around 50 cups of Chai, which after your first cup will seem like a breeze as this is such a delicious brew.

Makes 1 Large Jar, or approximately 50 drinks
500gm / 16½oz loose black tea, heaped
200gm / 6½oz drinking chocolate powder
¼ cup cloves
¼ cup star anise
¼ cup cinnamon, ground
¼ cup cardamom pods
¼ dry ginger, ground
2 vanilla pods, finely chopped

Add all the ingredients to a large jar and shake well.

chai tea - the brew

Makes 1 x 480ml / 14-16oz teapot or 4 drinks
2 tablespoons dry Chai tea
480ml / 14-16oz milk
¼ cup sugar

Stir all the ingredients in a large saucepan over a low heat. Continually stir to stop the milk from burning. Keep the ingredients simmering for about 5 minutes before ladling into cups through a tea strainer.

Once you start, you'll find it hard to stop. It's delicious.

tea sweet suggestions - by d'ough espresso

vienna ecclair buscuits

mini baked ricotta cheesecakes

mini nutty carrot cakes

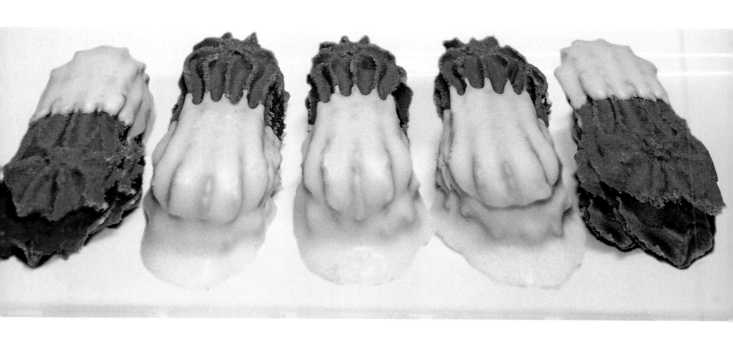

CCCCCCCCCCCCCCCCC
CCCCCCCCCCCCCCCCCCC

coffee

To keep this chapter of rational length and to the point, I will tell you a little about coffee. The real stuff comes from Colombia, Jamaica, Yemen, Kenya and Indonesia. That's not suggesting that all others are crap, they're probably just over-priced for what they are.

What you are looking for is 100% pure Arabica bean. The Robusta bean is grown at a lower altitude and therefore the cherry fruit from which the stone, or coffee been is derived, matures too quickly and becomes bitter in flavour.

As the fruit matures over a longer period of time, the acidity becomes more balanced with the bitterness resulting in a higher quality taste. Some regions like Yemen and Kenya are renown for producing Mocha coffee. This is not a mix of chocolate and coffee but a flavour produced from the bean that when roasted and ground produces a subtle chocolate flavour. It's very hard to get the original stuff from Yemen, and if you do be prepared to cut your right arm off for a handful of beans.

Percolators are the sworn enemy in the world of the black bean brew. They were primarily an American gadget that never has done justice to any coffee. The distinctive 'plurp plurp' sound of this washing machine style coffee cooker scorches the ground coffee repeatedly, exacerbating the bitterness, resulting in a bland flavour. So do yourself a favour and throw it out. The best method is the seal and heat drip pot, which are available in most appliance stores.

The home espresso or cappuccino machine
is a joyous asset to any kitchen.

To keep this simple I have included some basic coffee recipes plus some of my own perky variations.

early morning coffee and rocky road

milk constriction

Heat the milk in a jug with the steamer sunk deep into it. Place your hand under the jug to test the temperature of the milk which should be just over warm, not hot. Draw the steamer to the top of the warm milk and allow the milk to rise with the aeration. Keep this up until the base of the jug is hot to touch then leave the jug of hot aerated milk for about 10 seconds and tap the base of the jug to deflate any large air bubbles. Hold a saucer on top of the jug and pour the milk into a glass or cup. This allows the froth to mix consistently with the hot milk.

macchiato

A Macchiato is commonly served in a short black glass and in Italian means 'stained or spotted'. The term of being stained refers to being stained with the addition of milk, but not so as to make a white, milky drink. It can be served in three ways consisting of 30ml/1oz of espresso:

Freddo - stained with a teaspoon of cold milk.

Caldo - stained with a teaspoon of hot milk.

Frotho - stained by a heaped teaspoon of hot dense creamy froth served on top of the espresso.

café latte - flat white

The latte glass with a folded napkin on the side is the traditional way of serving this popular milky coffee. The Antipodean's version which is served in a ceramic cup has been named the 'flat white'.

ristretto - espresso - short black

The difference between the three is simply the quantity of coffee used in a short glass or demitasse cup. A Ristretto will use between 10-15ml/¼oz, an Espresso about 30ml/1oz, and the Short Black ironically has the most coffee at approximately 45ml/1½oz for a perfect serve.

The object here is to extract the pure essence of coffee where the natural coffee crema (the creamy brown froth on the surface of the coffee) is, in the case of the Ristretto, half the drink itself. This is real appreciation territory and the strength of these little drinks make them the perfect pick-me-up.

dominican espresso

Makes 1 drink
15ml / ½oz Cointreau
2 teaspoon sugar
orange rind
30ml / 1oz espresso, freshly drawn

Place orange rind and sugar in your glass, followed by the coffee and Cointreau. Stir bruising the rind. This allows more flavour to dissipate through brew.

golden marshmallow short black

Makes 1 drink
15ml / ½oz Galliano gold liqueur
1 teaspoon sugar
2 marshmallows
45ml / 1½oz espresso, freshly drawn

Add Galliano and sugar to a glass and stir until the sugar is dissolved. Add a marshmallow and pour the hot coffee over the ingredients. Allow the marshmallow to soften for a few minutes before devouring.

double espresso - doppio - long black

This is simply a double dose of coffee from a double pour handle served in a lattè glass or double cup. By running double the length of an espresso, being approximately 60ml/ 2oz, you are effectively getting twice the caffeine or as I say a 'double happy'. A long black coffee is 80-90ml/3oz of drawn coffee. All in all the similarities are far and few between, so I need to make a point of difference with these little hot numbers.

double trouble

This is the ultimate nightcap for a very groovy dinner party or a good excuse to avoid a dessert. There's nothing quite like a cup of trouble to get the conversation brewing.

Makes 1 drink
20ml / ¾oz Maker's Mark bourbon
2 teaspoon sugar
1 liquorice stick
30ml / 1oz espresso, freshly drawn
30ml / 1oz milk, heated

Stir sugar and Maker's Mark bourbon well in a glass. Add freshly brewed coffee and the milk then place the liquorice in. Stir the brew with the liquorice and alternate between drinking and chewing.

café bon bon

I fell in love with this drink in Spain where it was available in most cafés and tapas bars.

Makes 1 drink
30ml / 1oz condensed milk, sweetened
60ml / 2oz espresso, freshly drawn

Pour the espresso and add the condensed milk. It will sink to the bottom of your glass, creating a layered affect. Stir before drinking.

dominican espresso, golden marshmallow short black, double trouble, café bon bon

clove and vanilla flat white

Makes 1 drink

30ml / 1oz espresso coffee, freshly drawn

1 cup milk, frothed

2 drops vanilla extract, or half vanilla bean

3 cloves

sugar, to taste

Heat the cloves and vanilla with the milk in a frothing jug. Allow to stand before adding to coffee in a cup.

cappuccino

Made famous by its excentric and often absurdly frothy mountains, the Cappuccino represents the typical morning coffee one would enjoy in Italy. However, they make it vastly differently in Italy to the way it's made in other counties.

Firstly, the Italians would never dream of giving you a peaked white cumulus that looked like it just swallowed a lost weather balloon. Nor will they scoop the froth onto the coffee creating a separation.

A real Italian coffee will be very light in texture
and like a good fresh accompanying pastry it should melt in your mouth.

Makes 1 drink

30ml / 1oz espresso coffee, freshly drawn

1 cup milk, frothed

sugar, to taste

cocoa powder

Pour the espresso coffee into a cup and add frothed milk. Dust with cocoa powder.

roasted colombian arabica beans

café dakota

Dakota liqueur and coffee is a favourite of mine.

Makes 2 drinks
120ml / 4oz espresso coffee
120ml / 4oz hot milk
60ml / 2oz Dakota liqueur (see p 90)
1 tablespoon caster sugar

Fill each cup or glass with 60ml/2oz coffee. Pour the Dakota liqueur in with the milk and froth before adding to a glass. Garnish with a cinnamon stick.

café batido

Batido, Spanish for 'beaten', is a real treat and worth the effort. It's a very light soufflé style coffee that is best enjoyed as a dessert.

Makes 4 drinks
60ml / 2oz espresso, freshly drawn
2 eggs, white separated from the yolk
2 tablespoons caster sugar
1 teaspoon cinnamon

Beat the egg white with a whisk until stiff. Add the egg yolks and continue beating. Add sugar and cinnamon and coffee to the beaten egg mixture. The egg mixture should be light and fluffy.

Serve with teaspoons and garnish with cinnamon sprinkles.

woody and sunil having a laugh over a coffee

vienna coffee

The typical Vienna coffee is 60ml/2oz of fresh espresso and a large spoonful of whipped cream served in a large glass with a dusting of chocolate or cinnamon.

cognac snaps mocha coffee

The real mocha coffee is a wonderful blend of Yemen and Kenyan beans. For those who simply don't care about the beans they grind, I have added a great recipe for a spiced up cup of mocha.

Makes 1 drink
30ml / 1oz espresso, freshly drawn
30ml / 1oz Hennessy V.S cognac
1 teaspoon chocolate powder
2 teaspoon sugar
1 cup milk, frothed
1 tablespoon cream, freshly whipped

Mix up the chocolate powder, cognac, sugar and coffee to create a paste in the bottom of a tall highball glass. Pour over frothed milk and add a dollop of freshly whipped cream. Garnish with chocolate sauce on top or dust with chocolate powder.

iced coffee

Makes 1 drink

60ml / 2oz espresso, freshly drawn

120ml / 4oz milk, chilled

2 scoops vanilla ice cream

ice

Place a small amount of ice into the base of a tall glass with two scoops of vanilla ice cream. Pour the espresso on top and fill with cold milk. Top with whipped cream and dust with chocolate powder. Serve on a small plate with a long teaspoon and straw.

café beijing

Makes 1 drink

60ml / 2oz espresso, freshly drawn

120ml / 4oz milk, frothed

2 star anise

1 teaspoon allspice

sugar, to taste

Draw the coffee and pour into a bowl. Froth the milk with the allspice and star anise. Add to the bowl using the milk constriction method (see p 176).

café affogato

Affogato means 'drowned' in Italian. Although this refers to the ice cream being drowned, I frequently submerge my taste buds in one of these.

Makes 1 drink

60ml / 2oz hot espresso coffee

1 large scoop vanilla ice cream

Place a neat scoop of ice cream in a small bowl and pour piping hot espresso over the top.

coffee cake suggestions - by d'ough espresso

delicious layers of coffee flavoured meringue

black and white chocolate mouse cake

backed ricotta cheesecake covered with roasted almond flakes

kdkdkdkdkdkdkdkdkd
kdkdkdkdkdkdkdkdkd

kids' drinks

I always enjoy planning kids' parties where they get to try drink making themselves. Presenting a mob of thirsty kids with all the ingredients they'll need for a drinks party and letting them go for it is hilarious, and needless to say, they have a ball.

Just stand back with a large, fitted waterproof apron and give them pointers where not to pour the ingredients.

The drinks in this chapter are to give you a slice of this colourful experience - C.H.A.O.S (children hyped absolutely on sugar) . . . and some great ideas for your kids' party instead of laying out bottles of carbonated caffeine to get them fired up.

cranberry snowbear

Makes 1 drink

30ml / 1oz Ocean Spray Cranberry Classic juice

1 handful raspberries

1 handful strawberries, chopped

90ml / 3oz lemonade

2 teaspoon caster sugar

ice

Place the fruit into your highball glass and then pour the cranberry juice. Blend the lemonade and sugar with the ice and pour slowly ontop of the raspberry and cranberry mixture. The blended lemonade should form light coloured peaks.

Serve with long straws or long teaspoons.

fruit fantasy

Makes 1 drink

3 watermelon chunks

3 pineapple chunks

3 strawberries, pruned

1 teaspoon caster sugar

20ml / ¾oz sugar syrup (see p 25)

60ml / 2oz Ocean Spray Cranberry Classic juice

ice

Peel and roughly chop the watermelon and pineapple. Put the fruit into a glass and add one teaspoon of sugar and the sugar syrup. Crush the ingredients into a juicy mash with a French rolling pin (see p 41). Add ice and top with Ocean Spray Cranberry Classic.

kernal custard pie

Makes 2 drinks

300ml / 10oz cold milk

2 teaspoons vanilla essence

4 tablespoons honey

1 banana, chopped

1 egg yolk

1 nutmeg pinch

hundreds and thousands

Slowly pour some of the honey around the inside of the glass carefully turning the glass. Add the hundreds and thousands and turn the glass to coat the inside. Blend the first six listed ingredients until smooth and pour up in prepared glasses.

sebastian and laichlan making kernal custard pie

chocolate bomb

angel pie

This is without a doubt the single most popular kids' drink we have ever made. Kids just seem to love the flavour and because it is basically an alcohol free version of the Sahara (see p 78), kids feel like they are a part of the party too.

Makes 1 drink
30ml / 1oz strawberry purèe (see p 78)
30ml / 1oz lemon cordial
60ml / 2oz mango nectar
½ passionfruit
ice

Pack a large old-fashioned glass with ice and build the ingredients in the listed order. Squeeze passionfruit pulp on top of the drink for flavour and garnish purposes.

chocolate bomb

Considering that it's hard to find a kid that doesn't like chocolate, this is an exceptionally popular drink.

Makes 1 drink
100ml / 3½oz cold milk
1 tablespoon peanut butter
1 tablespoon honey
1 tablespoon cocoa powder
1 tablespoon sugar
ice

Heat the honey and cocoa powder in a microwave and stir together until smooth and no cocoa lumps remain. Pour the honey-cocoa mixture along with the milk and peanut butter to a blender with one scoop of ice. Blend until smooth. Garnish with chocolate topping (see p 36) and crushed nuts on the rim (see p 207).

greedy guts picnic pleaser

This is a real party pleaser and can be made as a punch in a large bowl.

Before you go on a picnic or excursion
allow at least one hour for the drink to infuse
the flavours of the snakes.

Makes 2Lt / 66½oz, or approximately 6 drinks
1Lt / 33½oz Ocean Spray Ruby Red Grapefruit juice
1 packet snake lollies
700ml / 23½oz ginger beer
ice

Add all the ingredients to a 2Lt / 66½oz bottle and top up with ice.

cookie monster

This is a fun drink all kids find irresistible. Who could say no to a cookie milkshake?

Makes 1 drink
90ml / 3oz cold milk
30ml / 1oz caramel syrup
1 chocolate buscuit
1 teaspoon vanilla essence
1 teaspoon sugar
ice

Blend all the ingredients with ice and serve with straws in a tall highball glass. Garnish with sprinkled nuts.

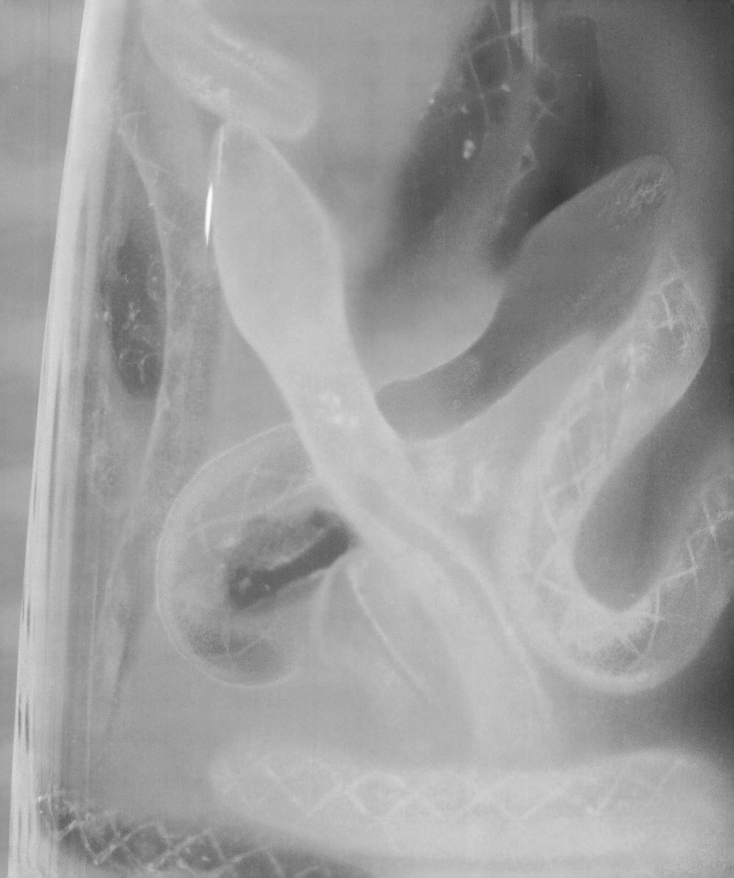

ice cream sandwich

This is a double blend drink, which makes a great swirly surprise for kids. They just love the colour combination.

Makes 4 drinks
4 large scoops ice cream
1 large mango
1 teaspoon vanilla essence
4 drops coconut essence
250ml / 8½oz plain yoghurt, unsweetened
4 tablespoons sugar
1 punnet strawberries
4 cups cold milk
ice

stage 1 - first blend

Blend the ice cream, mango, vanilla and coconut essence with two cups of fresh milk. Blend until smooth and then pour up in four long glasses.

stage 2 - second blend

Blend the yoghurt, strawberries and sugar with the remaining two cups of milk in a blender half filled with ice. Pour over the ice cream and mango mixture and garnish with a chocolate sauce web (see p 36).

sebastian, aaron, isabella and laichlan enjoy their creations

kids' drinks food suggestions - homemade pizzas

mushroom and roasted capsicum with tomato and capsicum relish on lebanese bread

roasted cherry tomato with pesto mayonaise and oregano leaves on cheese naan bread

king prawns with fresh basil leaves and vine ripened tomato on crispy tortillas

brand glossary

chambord

Made from rich black and red raspberries, sweetened cognac with vanilla and honey; Chambord is the finest berry liqueur in the world. Originating from France and best known for its versatility and mixability in cocktails, this stunning liqueur is widely known as the original liqueur in the Cosmopolitan cocktail. 16.5% Alc/Vol

cointreau

Made from bitter and sweet oranges from the Caribbean, Spain, Brazil and Peru. Cointreau's subtle taste originates from the blend of the orange fragrant peels which have been carefully selected for their quality. It is found in almost every bar in the world and is an essential liqueur in cocktails. 40% Alc/Vol

havana club silver dry

Silver Dry is the result of blending matured rums for at least 18 months. It is a light coloured rum, made from quality sugar cane alcohol, with a balanced full-flavour . Silver dry is the most popular mixable rum available. 40% Alc/Vol

havana club añejo reserva

Añejo Reserva is made with various Cuban rums of different ages. The use of young rums with more mature rums, give it a well-balanced, powerful taste. This makes Añejo Reserva an excellent cocktail spirit. 40% Alc/Vol

hennessy v.s

In 1865, Maurice Hennessy createded the Three Star Cognac, better known today as V.S. It makes for perfect mixing in cocktails such as the Sidecar. 40% Alc/Vol

imagin ...

Imagin is a sophisticated spirit and is flavoured like most gins with juniper berries. It has a clean flavour while still holding enough oomph to characterise any mixed drink with the unmistakable presence of a great gin. 40% Alc/Vol

jose cuervo especial

Jose Cuervo Especial is made from the Blue Agave plant. It is exceptionally smooth in taste with a hint of sweetness and has a rich, well-balanced character of oak, spices and vanilla tones. This is the number one selling tequila in the world and without a doubt makes the best Margarita. 38% Alc/Vol

maker's mark

A smooth sipping bourbon whisky that is sweeter than most other brands. Maker's Mark bourbon is an easy drinking spirit, perfect over ice or the ultimate whisky to mix in cocktails. 43% Alc/Vol

ocean spray ruby red grapefruit

Ocean Spray Ruby Red Grapefruit juice is a refreshing source of vitamin C and is naturally fat-free, cholesterol-free and very low in sodium. The citrus and crisp character and flavour allow it to be extremely popular in mixed drinks for all ages.

ocean spray cranberry classic

Ocean Spray Cranberry Classic juice is pleasantly tart and dry. It blends perfectly with a variety of other mixers and is available at almost every supermarket in a variety of bottle sizes. The one-of-a-kind cranberry taste is an excellent source of antioxidant vitamin C.

piper heidsieck

Piper Heidsieck Cuvée Brut champagne brings its own lively, vivacious and exuberant character to dry champagne. Brilliant on it's own and exquisite as a Piper Fruit cocktail. 12% Alc/vol

seriously ... vodka

A pure, clean and very crisp vodka that doesn't leave a burning hot sensation after drinking. It isn't oily in its flavour finish, therefore it is the ultimate cocktail spirit. 40% Alc/Vol

seriously ... pinky

Pinky is to vodka what Picasso is to art. Simply the most versatile flavoured vodka ever produced. Pinky is flower-powered alcohol, perfect for fruit based cocktails. It contains natural botanicals and has the subtle aroma of violets. 40% Alc/Vol

tips and tricks

egg white

Egg white is used for altering the texture and presentation of a drink when shaken. It is best stored in a squeeze bottle for easy dispensing. Be sure to add a little water to your egg white and shake vigorously to break up the globules before use. Egg white lasts one day.

finding equipment and stock

Most supermarkets stock all the dry and liquid ingredients. Bottle shops stock many of the quality spirits and liqueurs you will see listed in this book. For bar equipment you'll find it easy ordering through www.barequip.com

glass recycling

Eventually you are going to wind up with a whole heap of dirty glasses. So make a round with someone to pick up the empties. Give them a wash and put them back at your drink making station.

ice

Bags of ice can be bought from any service station and most bottle shops. Never scoop ice with a glass as they can break, which means the ice can't be used and the whole mess needs to be cleaned up straight away for safety. Ideally use a cocktail shaker, a plastic scoop or plastic cup (see p 14).

jammed cocktail shaker

If your cocktail shaker has contracted with the cold shaking of the ice and you can't unseal any of the three-piece shaker, then try pouring a little hot water from the tap over the cap to help it expand and open. If it's a Boston shaker that is giving you grief, try tapping the stainless steal shaker gently on the edge of the bench while holding both ends.

knowing when enough is enough

Failing to heed the tell-tale signs that you are reaching your limit will inevitably wipe you out following a night in your liquid kitchen. This is different for everyone due to their body size and tolerance to alcohol. Proportionally, the average adult male can consume one standard drink every hour and burn this off to be sober enough to drive. An adult woman on the other hand can consume approximately a third less than a man and remain sober. My best tip is to make sure you eat, drink water regularly throughout the night and preferably get a taxi home.

making mistakes

This is really the best way to get ahead in your liquid kitchen. Just dive head first into the abyss of do's and don'ts and eventually surface for air when the blender needs refilling. If you are making an abundance of blunders perhaps you need to think of it this way... dignity is something that cannot be preserved in alcohol.

matching drinks with food

Coffee and cake is a classic example of a perfect union. At the end of each chapter you can find our friends' suggestions of what to serve with the listed drinks. Let's face it, alcohol normally makes people feel hungry. So always make sure that there is plenty of food available for your guests to eat as there is nothing more embarrassing than having hungry guests raiding your fridge.

pouring and measuring

If you don't have a pourspout or a jigger (spirit measure) you might like to improvise with a good old eggcup. The average eggcup holds approximately 45ml/1½oz. It's always a good idea to try it out before starting. Measuring by sight is rarely consistent so use my rule of thirds for the majority of mixed drinks in this book: One third alcohol and two thirds mixers always makes a well balanced cocktail.

recovery preparation

Thinking ahead is by far the best way to minimise the damage control of a seedy morning. Drinking four large glasses of water before going to bed accompanied by a Vitamin B and more water when you rise will help get rid of your hangover, which is a result of dehydration from alcohol.

Funny isn't it? We actually dehydrate ourselves while we drink alcohol, but that's just the way it goes. In the morning a good swim will wash away the cobwebs from behind the ears and if all else fails - stay in bed and try not to move too much. This followed by some groaning can help a lot, maybe a little moaning and a bit of panting. You might even induce some pity… but then again you might not!

rimming your glass

Rimming your glass can be a glamorous way of garnishing cocktails or drinks. It can also form a crucial part of the flavour. A classic Margarita with the all-important salt rim is like an unmistakable serving of fish 'n' chips. Without the salt, the flavour lacks character and slips back into the realm of 'it's missing something?'

To rim your glass with salt or sugar, rub the rim of the glass with a slice of lime or lemon and then dust the rim into a plate of the ingredient of your choice. For more textured ingredients such as nuts or coconut, use honey instead of a citrus fruit as this will help the garnish attach better.

running out of ingredients

Be adventurous and improvise with other ingredients you may have available. If you have run out of alcohol then perhaps retiring for the night at your local watering hole is a good way of avoiding the situation.

serving suggestions

By following the recipes and methods listed in The Liquid Kitchen you shouldn't have any trouble making any of the drinks. Substituting any of the ingredients in the recipes is all part of the evolution of cocktail making. If you have any new recipes or drink ideas that are winners please feel free to leave them in the guest book section of our website: www.mondobartender.com

wet floors

Thinking about it, slipping over on a wet floor is probably the number one danger in any home drink maker's party. If drinks are being prepared and plenty of people are using your kitchen keep an old towel or two handy for use on the floor.

thankyou, thankyou, thankyou

I would like to thank the following people for all their help, contributions and expertise. Patience, suggestions, encouragement and patronage will never go unnoticed. Your thoughtfulness, love and devotion will always be remembered. Much love and happiness to you all and thanks for everything.

Hayden Wood, AKA Woody.

Esmeralda Wood for your wonderful photography and design, Steven MacDonald for your focus and direction, Paula Opfer, Gaelene and Sam Adams Wood, Sunil Budami, Carron Ikin, Stuart Johnston, Blair Johnstone, Michael Filler, Tony Curtis, Leonie Curtis, Mario Rosslind, Belinda Boog, Sebastian Wright, Laichlan Wright, Aaron Valenti, Isabella Valenti, Lyndey Milan from The Australian Women's Weekly, Trudi Jenkins from delicious. Magazine, George Maniatis from Spinninghead, Richard Cooper from Tomkin Australia, Belinda Lyone from Suntory Australia, Ann-Marie Ogilvie from Ocean Spray, Ray Noble and John Coles from Swift and Moore, Antoine Garnier from Maxxium France, Sara Black and Simon Graham from Maxxium Australia, Carla Seaton from Drink City International, Rob Cooper from Chambord, Paul Wilson from Orlando Wyndham, Fiona Wilson from Tower Books, Bill Honeybone from Celebrity Books, Sean Semler from Topan Printing, Photo Garden in Newtown, Pia and Martin from Art on King Newtown, Marianne from T2 Newtown, Damion Alves and Will Young from Campos Coffee Newtown.

Thanks heaps to the contributors who gave up their time, food stock and accessories to compliment the drinks in The Liquid Kitchen.

Longrain Restaurant and Bar - 85 Commonwealth St, Surry Hills, NSW 2010 - www.longrain.com.au

Bayswater Brasserie - 32 Bayswater Rd, Kings Cross, NSW 2011 Tel: (02) 9357-2177 www.bayswaterbrasserie.com.au

Katering - 02 9319 2700 www.katering.com.au

Cherry Bim - Kosher Caterers 02 9488 7222 www.cherrybim.com

Lyndey Milan - Author of Lyndey Milan's Fabulous Food - (pp 38-39, 56-57, 62-63) Available through www.amazon.com

Sabor de España - 153a King Street, Newtown, NSW 2042 Tel: 02 9519 1313

D'ough Espresso - 257a King Street, Newtown, NSW 2042 Tel: 02 9557 3476

T2 - Tea accessories 173 King Street, Newtown, NSW 2042 Tel: 02 9550 3044

Barequip.com - www.barequip.com Tel: 1300 301 107

MONDO Bartender Training - www.mondobartender.com Tel: 02 9565 2566

To my family and friends. Sorry for neglecting you through the production of this project. Thanks for your understanding and support. I will try and make it up to you somehow.

Thank you to all the wonderful clients of MONDO across Australia and the world, also the Jewish community in Sydney who have embraced our business. You all drink zillions of our cocktails every year and this keeps the dream alive. To my incredible staff at MONDO that make this madness happen. Every event is always a blast with you guys and girls . . . thanks a gazillion!

All that I can, I can be,
all that we can, we can see.

index

Italicized numbers refer to photographs.